The MBA Distilled for Project & Program Professionals

The MBA Distilled for Project & Program Professionals

Up-Level Your Skills & Career by Mastering the Best Parts of an MBA Program

Bradley D. Clark

BUSINESS EXPERT PRESS

Leader in applied, concise business books

This book is dedicated to my beautiful wife, Colleen, who is the author of all the good things in my life.

Description

Certifications in project management are like birthdays: everybody has one. These days, you need something more to distinguish yourself in this profession. This book is a practical guide for project and program managers who want to increase their professional skills by incorporating relevant theory, formulas, and other learnings from the Master of Business Administration (MBA) curriculum. The book provides an overview of core classes taught in most MBA programs, but with a specific lens on how to make the material practical for project practitioners.

The book starts with strategy, and works its way through economics, finance, operations, leadership, and other core areas. Each chapter introduces the reader to fundamental subject matter, then brings it to life in terms and experiences that resonate with project and program managers. Real-world challenges and experiences are shared to bolster the relevance of the material being taught.

Project and program managers will learn new tools to improve critical decision making, formulas and techniques for making recommendations to leadership, and an assortment of theories and techniques for up leveling their management skills with teams and stakeholders.

The book concludes with a fresh and honest look at whether the reader would benefit from pursuing an MBA themselves. It helps the reader understand the benefits and challenges associated with pursuing an MBA. Finally, it helps the reader determine whether an MBA is right for the reader at all, and if so, what type of MBA program would be the best to pursue based on the reader's own circumstances.

Keywords

project management; program management; career advancement; management; project; program; career; business; process; value; decision; analysis; change; people; advancement; MBA; market; employees; analysis; risk; professional; financial; benefits; promotion; analysis; skills; tools

Contents

Preface

I remember the day I was accepted into the Evening and Weekend MBA program at U.C. Berkeley's Haas School of Business (Haas). I had applied to three other schools in case Haas didn't want me. In my mind, I'd just hit the lottery. Haas was a top 20 MBA program, and the Evening and Weekend program was in the top three. I had a feeling that I had just caught a tiger by the tail, and I was right. Haas was rigorous, intense, and costly.

There are a lot of reasons to pursue an MBA. Some do it to advance in the career they are in. Some do it to learn entrepreneurship. Still others want to switch careers. I was toying with the idea of becoming an entrepreneur. I felt I was stagnating in my project career, and I just didn't know if I had the passion to stay with it for several more decades. The MBA delivered a lot of benefits, chief among them was a first-class ticket to understanding the way all parts of modern business run. It also helped me clarify that—at that time of my life—I would have been a terrible entrepreneur. I avoided a big pitfall, and I am grateful for what I learned. It also helped be become a better project manager because it exposed me to so much business knowledge that could be applied to my project management practice.

This kind of knowledge came at a cost. The time commitment was enormous. I missed out on three years of watching kids grow up. My wife paid a price by shouldering the burden of being a Haas widow. The bill for this privilege was north of $80k. Was it worth it? Yes, but. The *but* is why I wrote this book. What I do know is that the tools and strategies I learned have been and continue to be of tremendous value both professionally and personally. It is my goal to share with you the highest value learnings for a much lower cost than I had to pay. It is also my goal to arm those considering an MBA with the information they need to make the right decision for themselves.

I have been managing projects, programs, people, and PMOs for more than two decades. In this book, I will distill the most important elements of a typical MBA to those of us who practice project and program management. Not everything in an MBA program is of importance to project and program managers, but some of the knowledge can help project professionals rise to new levels in our profession.

Introduction

Most MBA programs don't talk much about project management. To them, it's a tactical necessity to achieve a strategic end. In my career, I've learned that shrewd business leaders understand that a strong project management function is as critical as any of the other functions taught in an MBA program. What MBA program teach can make us better at what we do. Combining the skills of project and program management with those of an MBA gives us a broader professional range from tactical to strategic.

This book covers the courses in a typical MBA core curriculum. Chapters 1 through 9 will cover one class each. Chapter 1 will focus on strategy, the heart of every business. Subsequent chapters will work through the other classes, as shown in Figure I.1.

Within each chapter, I will introduce key concepts and terminology related to the subject under study. The concepts will be broad because there is no way to pack an entire MBA course into a chapter. Once the subject basics have been outlined, the chapter will cover those parts that crossover into the project management world. Each chapter will examine concepts and tools that can be adopted to and improve your professional toolset. The book covers decision-making theories, financial analyses, business accounting concepts, and much more.

This book uses the word *distilled* on purpose. It's not possible to cover two years of rigorous academic teaching in a single book. You won't be earning any degrees at the end of the book, but you *will* come away with an understanding of what I consider the choicest parts of an MBA program. Better yet, you will be introduced to new skills that, with a little practice, can be applied to your projects right now. I wish I could promise mastery just by reading, but these are complex topics that take regular MBA students concentrated lectures, homework, and study to master. As such, I have included links to additional resources to help you continue your studies. My website www.mbadistilled.com is also a great resource as you continue your studies.

Strategic Core
Strategy defines organizational direction. All other functions take their signals from organizational strategy

Language of Business
Organizations use financial language to describe their success. Understanding and speaking that language is important to organizational and professional success

Supporting Functions
Organizations cannot function without marketing, operations, and other key functions that support the growth and function of the organization

People Layer
People are the engine that powers organizations. Wrapped around the other disciplines, people functions help unleash the potential within people

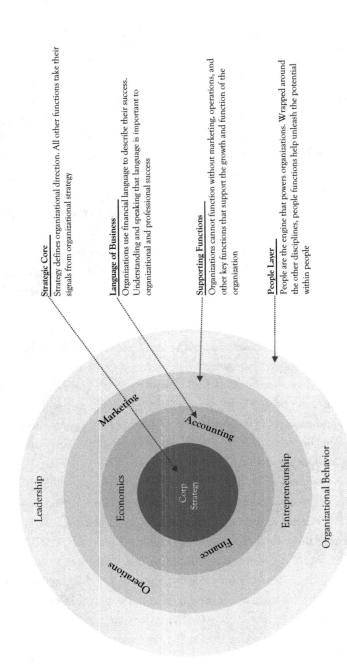

Figure I.1 Hierarchy of MBA core topics in this book

Chapter 10 is designed to help anyone considering entering business school. I share ideas about who will most benefit from an MBA, what tier of school is right for you, and what you can honestly expect if you decide to get your degree.

Who Will Benefit From This Book?

I wrote this book with a few types of reader in mind. My target audience is of course those who are in project and program management, but the information covered and the tools and techniques demonstrated are applicable to anyone.

Early Career Project Management Professional

The tools and techniques taught in this book will increase your professional toolkit and give you concepts you can immediately apply in your work. I try to use the tools demonstrated in this book whenever applicable in my work—but I don't see these tools commonly used by others. I believe if you can master even a few of these, you will be able to add substantial value and gain positive attention within your organization.

Additionally, this book can help you find clarity as to whether you should pursue an MBA in your own life. Those who know they want it will be guided to choose the type of MBA right for them. Those who are unsure they want to pursue an MBA should find more clarity about the decision. Those who've never considered an MBA may have their mind opened to an exciting possibility they had not considered.

Be clear, though, I do not recommend MBA programs for everyone. In the last chapter you will learn what it is like in an MBA program, but more importantly, who is likely to benefit the most. It is my goal to help you determine for yourself the right course of action. For some, mastering the concepts introduced in this book will be enough to propel them forward in their career.

Mid-Career Project Management Professional

For those who have been executing projects for a number of years, this book can help in a couple of ways. First, for those who want to remain an individual contributor but take on larger or more complex work, this book will introduce you to techniques and tools that, when mastered, will prove you can manage more complex work. As you petition management for more complex work, you will be able to demonstrate a broader set of skills. Better yet, you can demonstrate these skills in real life in the project work you're already doing.

For those who are considering moving into a Program Management Office (PMO) leadership role, even more of the tools and techniques will apply. Demonstrating mastery of these concepts will help your case as you move forward on the leadership path.

PMO Leaders

Many of the tools and techniques demonstrated in this book apply to the kinds of problems a PMO leader needs to solve, especially as you look across an entire portfolio of work. These tools can help you optimize resources, clarify priorities, and estimate value. These tools can help you transform your PMO from a tactical execution team to a strategic value-generation organization. It can also help you bolster your credibility in your organization because your colleagues in other departments will recognize your elevated professionalism.

Ultimately, we all must show the value of the work we do. PMO leaders have the added burden of showing the value of all the work under their management. Employing these tools and techniques will assist you with that because you will be speaking the language of business.

Anyone Considering an MBA

This book is a high-level survey of the core MBA curriculum covered in typical business schools. Woven throughout the chapters are insights into MBA curriculum that will give you a glimpse of what to expect if you decide to go in that direction. I lay out my reasoning around who will benefit most and least so that it provides guidance as you make your choice. You do not need to be a project or program manager to use these insights as part of your decision making.

Conventions and Considerations

- Throughout this book, I use the term *project and program manager* as a way to capture all the roles dedicated to project and program delivery—from the greenest associate project manager to the most experienced PMO executive. I am not aware of a single term in our profession that covers all of these roles.

- At the end of each chapter, I give you options for further study. Given that the textbooks used in MBA-level classes can be hundreds of dollars (each), I have looked at open/free texts and other resources that are high quality and of sufficient depth to help you, should you want to learn more. In most instances, I was pleasantly surprised by the quality of the freely available texts.

- I do not refer you to any specific in-person or online training on the concepts covered in this book because I am hesitant to vouch for any resource I am not familiar with, and I have not taken any of these courses.

- MBA students are encouraged to absorb themselves in business discussions, news, and culture. Reading current and classic business books is highly encouraged for anyone serious about their career. Reading general business magazines and news sites such as *economist.com, newsweek.com, wsj.com,* and *ft.com* are also a great place to start.

CHAPTER 1

Corporate Strategy

Why Study Corporate Strategy?

Corporate strategy answers the most fundamental questions any organization has to consider. It is the organization's north star that guides the direction of the organization. Without a coherent and cohesive strategy, an organization will likely get distracted by its many opportunities and never gain the benefits of strong, focused attention in key strategic areas. Some of the key questions that strategy answers include:

- What are the organization's vision, mission, and values?
- In which markets should it compete?
- How should it compete in these markets?
- What is the organization's competitive advantage?

When answering the preceding questions, corporate strategists are really trying to figure out how the organization should position itself in the marketplace. There are many forces the organization can directly control (such as vision, mission, values), but there are significant competitive forces that the organization cannot directly control; thus, leadership must analyze and choose the right industry and approach to entering that industry in order for the organization to remain financially viable.

It is the role of project and program managers to help an organization bring life to projects that support strategy. Project and program managers are *executioners* of work that delivers strategic value to the organization. When the project management function in an organization increases its own maturity to the point it can help the organization prioritize its portfolio of work, it is filling a key strategic function. Understanding corporate strategy fundamentals will help you improve the project and program management function in your organization.

Understanding the Basics

The most critical role of corporate strategy is to set the overall direction the organization should pursue. This is done by setting the vision, mission, and values for the organization. The corporate strategy team should be active in managing corporate direction as well as investment of the organization's limited resources. It is important to note that the vision, mission, and values are typically stable over months and years, whereas priorities can change rapidly as circumstances shift.

It is almost cliché today to talk about an organization's vision and mission—but these two statements are among the most important strategic documents in the entire organization. When we couple the vision and mission with a set of strong values, the company has a foundation for building a strong organizational culture—and strong culture can be a real strategic advantage.

Vision Statement

An organization's vision statement should present an aspirational future state from which employees and shareholders can get inspiration. It gives the organization direction and sets broad goals for the organization to reach. Vision statements may sound like management gibberish, but if they are done with sincerity, they signal to all what top leadership hopes to accomplish. It should be a statement that employees rally around.

Mission Statement

A mission statement varies from a vision statement, in that there is more immediacy and direction for the work the organization will be doing and for whom. Some mission statements declare the market or customer they are targeting, some talk about the product they make or the service they provide. Some talk more about how they will get there. A mission statement should provide direction for the organization and allow employees and managers to focus attention on the right targets. Like vision statements, they should be succinct.

Values

The values an organization chooses to espouse can be very telling about the way they operate. Values are guardrails for how an organization operates. When taken seriously, they are one of the most important elements to guide employee and management behavior. Typically, organizations will adopt multiple values. They are sometimes called *core values*, and they are often shared publicly as a powerful marketing device.

The trick with values, as with vision and mission statements, is how sincerely the organization adopts them. I have been in organizations where these statements are merely corporate window dressing and are, thus, useless. I have also been in organizations where values are respected and obsessively followed. A company that lives its values can build a very strong company culture. A strong culture helps its workers to grow from transactional employees that are doing it for the paycheck, to invested employees who are empowered by the vision, mission, and values.

My advice is to try to work for organizations that have strong core values and an employee-friendly culture. In general, they will provide their employees with a better experience and more opportunities for career satisfaction. As project and program managers, it is more satisfying to contribute to the success of an organization that is empowered by a noble mission and strong values than by one that gives only surface attention to these strategic corporate documents.

I've also found that if you can tie the outcomes of your project(s) to the organization's overall vision or mission, you can improve your team's emotional involvement in the work. It can also be a powerful tool for helping keep focus and priority on the work of your project when there are other projects competing for the same resources.

Managing Priorities

Another major function of corporate strategy is to prioritize where the organization will focus its resources. Will the organization focus on expanding its current offering, or start a new product line? Will it grow its domestic base or open international offices? Will it spend more on product development or customer support? As stated earlier, unlike the vision, mission, and value statements, priorities change frequently with market dynamics.

Organization leadership regularly wrestles with large decisions that affect the direction in which the organization will head. Depending on the financial position of the organization, the vision and mission, and the macro and micro economic climates, leadership will focus the company on the priorities that make the most sense at the moment. Clearly, organizations are not able to pursue every opportunity, so they must sort through the many options to focus on a select few.

Leadership can draw on several tools to help sort priorities. In a mature organization, they would build business cases, run financial analyses like net present value (NPV), and then prioritize those options with the greatest potential payoff. Prioritization at the portfolio level helps manage this strategic prioritization step. Developing the project management function to operate at this strategic level is the ultimate expression of project management and should be the goal of all project organizations.

Some organizations are not mature enough to use business cases with extensive financial analysis. For these organizations, it is helpful to compare the importance and timeliness of the option against the effort and risk of doing it. By constructing a few questions for each measure, you can then develop a two-by-two matrix to categorize the options into actionable groups. Those that are most important and are the least effort would, of course, be prioritized highest. Those that are less important and most effort or risk would never be seriously considered for funding.

In project and program management, we often talk about managing risk as part of our project stewardship. When we talk this way, we inevitably mean identifying and managing negative risks. The truth is that some risks are positive. If you are involved in projects where you're helping create a product, there could be discovery or advancement potential seen during product development that could lead to new products or significant advancements of current ones. Identifying, tracking, and finding ways to exploit these positive risks can and should influence an organization's priorities.

Allocation of Resources

All resources in an organization can be broken down into dollars and cents. In many organizations planning is broken into two general categories: employees (labor) and budget dollars. Once top priorities are determined, the way they will be staffed and funded becomes the next priority. If the organization has identified an opportunity that they don't have the skills to pursue internally, they will either need to hire or purchase those skills to accomplish this priority. If they do have the talent, they will need to decide how many people to commit to the priority, given the other priorities that have also been approved.

Project and program managers have special skills in planning and managing resources and thus should attempt to find a place at the strategic table to assist leadership in defining the resourcing plans for these initiatives.

How Companies Strategically Compete

One of the fundamental strategic questions all companies must answer is how they will compete in the marketplace. What will their competitive advantage be? It is not possible to produce the most innovative product while also being the most cost effective and having the best customer support. Many marketing campaigns try to leave the impression that their product does all three things well—but it rarely ever happens. Companies tend to focus on one of three key strategic areas:

- Product leadership
- Cost leadership
- Customer intimacy

Product Leadership

A company that competes based on product leadership will invest money and resources into making and keeping their products cutting-edge and feature-rich. They will do research and development, or they will acquire innovative companies in the same space so that they can advance their product feature sets. Their marketing materials will play up their product leadership. Their products will not compete on price or on strong customer service. They will have to be adequate in each of those two areas, but product leadership will be their competitive advantage.

Think about Tesla. They lead the market in electric automobiles. There is a growing list of competitors out there, but when you think of Tesla, you think of innovation. Tesla has based its reputation on product innovation and leadership compared to their competitors, Tesla automobiles tend to be expensive, but that does not stop Tesla from selling as many vehicles as they can manufacture.

Cost Leadership

A company that competes on cost leadership is driven by efficiencies. Whether it is trading off product features to speed production or limiting options to keep manufacturing streamlined, it will produce competitive products at as low a price as it can manage. While it must offer adequate customer support, it will only provide enough support to keep it competitive, and they will not be innovating in their product area. Often, they will let the product leader do the innovation, then in the next product cycle or two, they will mimic the new features in their own product.

Cost leadership is easily seen in the airline industry. Airlines such as Spirit, Allegiant, and Ryanair are known for no-frills flying. They differentiate by rolling back features the rest of us assume will be part of a normal flight. A small snack and overhead compartment space were once standard amenities, but these airlines stripped features like these out of their standard offerings to become cost leaders in their markets. These low-feature airlines have set correspondingly low expectations for their customer service as well. Due to their low-profit, high-volume business, they cannot afford to innovate or provide white glove customer service. Whenever possible, customer interactions are pushed to phone apps and Internet portals.

Customer Intimacy

A company that competes on customer intimacy is all about making the customer feel special. Whether they target a very specific type of customer or they invest extensive resources on training and customer service, they sell an experience along with (sometimes) a product.

The quintessential service-focused company is the Nordstrom department store. They sell products that can be found in other stores, and they have typically limited their discounting practices, so how have they built such a loyal following? By offering superior service. When you purchase from Nordstrom, you can be confident they will stand behind the product by offering a generous return policy.

Nordstrom would not have its customer service reputation if it tried to be good at all three strategic areas (product leadership, cost leadership, and customer service). Their focus and resources would be diluted, and they would potentially be middling in all areas. Over time, other more focused companies would take over their market share. Thus, organization leaders must be strong enough to make strategic decisions about what direction the company will take and how it will compete in the market place.

Analyzing Competition: Porter's Five Forces

In 1980, Harvard Business School professor Michael E. Porter published his book, *Competitive Strategy: Techniques for Analyzing Industries and Competitors*[1] that contained a groundbreaking way of thinking about how competitive forces work in any industry. These five identified forces quickly became a backbone of corporate and business strategy. Understanding the forces at work in an organization's chosen industry is key to understanding how that organization can compete in that industry.

Conducting a competitive analysis will help an organization understand how much power the organization has, or could have, in an industry. We will review each of Porter's five forces in the following sections.

Competition in the Industry

When analyzing competition in an industry, we look at the number of competitors, their relative strength, and the number of products and services provided in the industry. When an industry has many competitors with strong positions in the market, breaking into that industry and remaining profitable will be difficult, and an organization's power in the industry will be diminished. A company entering an industry with a low amount of competition will have a better chance of building an effective competitive moat to keep out further competition. The problem is that industries with low competition are hard to find or are structurally difficult in which to be profitable. Any industry with an opportunity for high profits will attract a lot of competition, and with each new competitor, profitability in the industry will go down.

Potential for New Entrants

To understand whether a market is easy or difficult for a competitor to enter, we need to understand the concept of *barriers to entry*. Barriers to entering a market can be financial, physical, copyright or patent, government restriction, and more. Think about a company that wants to become an oil producer. There are substantial barriers to entering the market, including finding and purchasing drilling locations, government restrictions on drilling locations, and fluctuating oil costs that can quickly turn the industry unprofitable. A new entrant to the industry will have almost no ability to influence any of those barriers, so must accept them as realities if they choose to enter the market.

On the flip side are industries with almost no barriers to entry. Think about restaurants or neighborhood markets. These businesses come and go frequently because it does not take much to enter the market. A little knowledge and capital and anyone can jump in and give it a go. This low barrier to entry is attractive to new players, but is also one of the biggest challenges to existing organizations. Building a competitive advantage in a market where there are low barriers to entry is very difficult. This is why businesses that enter into these markets are often short-lived.

Power of Suppliers

If an industry has multiple suppliers, the ability to switch between suppliers is high, and the power of the suppliers is low. On the other hand, when an industry has few suppliers, an organization's dependency on the limited number of suppliers is high. The ability to freely switch between suppliers is low, making the power of suppliers high. An industry where suppliers have a lot of power is more challenging for market participants. Not only can suppliers control input costs to an organization, they can cripple the industry if supply chains become disrupted.

During the Covid-19 pandemic, the hand sanitizer industry experienced challenges keeping up with demand.[2] In addition to capacity challenges, the manufacturers of hand sanitizers were dependent on a limited number of isopropyl alcohol manufacturers who could not keep up with the demand. This caused a spike in costs to the manufacturers, as well as a fair amount of competition that used substitute products such as methyl alcohol to create competing products. It turned out that the methyl alcohol-based sanitizers were dangerous, and government regulation took those competitors out of the market, but during the supply crunch, the power of the isopropyl alcohol manufacturers spiked and costs to consumers jumped accordingly.

It's not just the number of suppliers that affects the power suppliers wield. Switching costs and availability of substitutes can affect the market too. Think about the contracts that exist between suppliers and producers. In the airline business, carriers like to lock in fuel costs at the lowest rates possible. In times of increasing fuel costs, an airline may lock in a rate that eventually, when fuel costs start to go down again, commits them to uncompetitive rates. This creates a challenge to the airlines as they fight to keep their ticket prices competitive.

Power of Customers

Sometimes, when we think about the power of customers, we think in terms of the common household purchasing power, but this is a narrow way of thinking about an organization's customer. Often, manufacturers' real customers are industry channels or retail outlets. One of the best ways to see the power of the customer is in the retail markets. Assume a new consumer product manufacturer wants to get its products to the broadest sets of consumers possible. To do this, it will have to go through major retail outlets such as Wal-Mart, Amazon, and Costco. How much power do you think the manufacturer will have in negotiations with these firms? Not much. These retailers are known for driving very difficult terms with their suppliers. The firm may search for alternative ways to reach the market, but those are limited. They can sell directly through their website, go through television infomercials, or other methods that are not nearly as effective as having shelf-space with prime retailers.

The buying power of customers is also high when the availability of competing products is abundant. If you manufacture a product that is easily produced by others, it will be hard for you to drive beneficial terms with your customers. You will need to find ways to differentiate your product within the market in order to get leverage with your customers.

Threat of Substitute Products

The fifth and final competitive force corporate strategists must consider is the power of substitute products. The more easily a customer can find a reasonable substitute product, the less power a supplier has in the marketplace. Conversely, the harder it is to find a substitute for your product, the more power you have in the industry.

An example of this power can be seen in the way people travel. If a person needs to get from one city to another, there are many substitutes. They can drive their car, a friend's car, or rent a car. They can take a bus, a train, or maybe an airplane. They could take a taxi, or a ride-sharing service. They could even ride a bicycle or walk. This means that the substitution power in this industry is high, making it hard for suppliers to set prices and drive profit for their organization.

BCG Matrix

The final strategic model we will look at in this chapter is the Boston Consulting Group (BCG) matrix, or growth–share matrix. This model was developed by the founder of BCG, Bruce D. Henderson, in the 1970s as a strategic tool to help customers know where to focus their product strategies.[3] Depending on the matrix category the investment falls into, an organization would be guided to invest more or less in that area.

The BCG matrix is a two-by-two grid with market share (high/low) along the x-axis and growth (high/low) along the y-axis. This results in a four-box grid, with each box representing a suggested action for the organization. This simple but powerful matrix allows organizations to map their product offerings to one of the four quadrants, each with tried and true industry suggestions for how to treat the product line to maximize value. It is important to understand that products can and do move from quadrants based on market and organization dynamics. Organizations should actively work to move their products to the best quadrants.

Each quadrant is briefly described as follows:

Star (upper-left quadrant): These are typically market leading products returning high return on investment (ROI). While these products have an enviable position, an organization must continually invest in the product to keep market position as other products are maneuvering to take the throne. As part of the normal product lifecycle, a star-level product may eventually become a cash cow.

Cash cow (lower-left quadrant): A product that is a cash cow is also in an enviable position as it has large market share, but in a low-growth industry. This quadrant is typically for products that have been on the market for a long time, likely with previous time in other quadrants. The goal with these products is to harvest as much profit from them without harming the brand.

Dog (lower-right quadrant): These products are in low-growth markets and have low market share. Unless there is a clear and direct path to improving the market share or market growth, the organization should purge these from their portfolios.

Question mark (upper-right quadrant): This quadrant is also sometimes called the *problem child* because products in this quadrant will require investment to move to the star quadrant, but there is no guarantee they will make the leap and could drop to the dog square. These products are often, but not necessarily, new.

While a project and program manager may not be making decisions around investment strategies for products, they may be involved in product revamp projects, new product introductions, and other similar efforts that impact an organization's strategic positioning. Understanding the company's strategy, and the place of your project in achieving that strategy, can be a valuable motivator for yourself and your team.

SWOT Analysis

Corporate strategists also use a tool called SWOT analysis. SWOT analysis can be applied to aspects of project and program management. SWOT analysis is a commonly used strategic analysis tool that examines internal

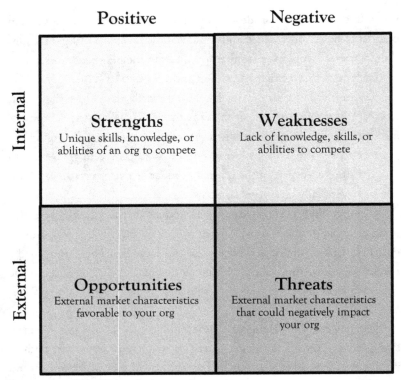

Figure 1.1 SWOT analysis template

and external factors impacting a company. It also analyzes the organization's inherent strengths and weaknesses. SWOT stands for strength, weakness, opportunity, threat, and each of these factors is mapped into a two-by-two grid to aid the analysis. Look at a typical SWOT analysis in Figure 1.1.

SWOT analysis is intended to be a quick but powerful way to examine an organization's strategic realities. It should not take weeks to assemble, but it should be more than a hastily put together document with little thought behind it. When creating a SWOT, be sure you have representatives from all areas of the organization involved. With skilled facilitation, there should be a general alignment achieved across all areas in a relatively short amount of time. Some organizations are so diversified that creating a single SWOT for the overall organization can be challenging. In those circumstances, it may be helpful to do SWOT analysis for the subdivisions as a starting place for the overall corporate analysis.

Strengths

An organization's strengths are the internal capabilities it has developed and can use to compete in the marketplace. Any analysis should include its competitive advantage, plus any unique capabilities it has based on its people, process, and technology.

When developing the list of organizational strengths, think carefully about what makes the organization unique. I recommend looking at people, process, and technology as buckets for your differentiation. What unique skills and abilities does your workforce have? Do you have any exclusive relationships that give you preferred access to a unique talent pool? Are your processes more efficient than competitors? Have they earned industry recognition, or are they recognized as industry best practice? What internal systems have you set up to run your business? Are you running the latest software, enabling you to maneuver more quickly as market circumstances change? Or, are you tied to old technology that locks you into existing processes?

Weaknesses

An organization's weaknesses are the internal capabilities that are still weak or nascent in the organization. As you've observed competitors, what have they been able to do that your organization has not? Looking across people, process, and technology—here are some questions to ask when doing the analysis: What key skillsets are you lacking? What organizational weaknesses are impacting your competitiveness in the marketplace? Is there overhead or weakness in your processes that is impacting your ability to compete? Are you burdened with old, inflexible technology or excessive technical debt? Call these out in the analysis.

Opportunities

Opportunities are external considerations that, if the organization can activate them, will increase its market position. These are positive risks. When listing opportunities, think about the marketplace and changes you are witnessing within it. Is the overall market growing? Are there new niches growing that you can focus on? Are markets converging, creating opportunities to branch into new areas? Are there technological advances taking place in your market (or in adjacent markets) that you can adopt to solidify your position? How are consumer or purchasing trends impacting the market? Again, call these out in the analysis.

Threats

As with opportunities, these are external factors that could, if they materialize, impact your organization negatively. Some threats could wipe you and your competitors out of the market if they are disruptive enough. When thinking of threats, look for disruptive technologies. What new products are emerging that may be *good enough* for consumers, but are offered in a radically less expensive or more impactful way. Think about new competitors, or competitors in adjacent markets expanding into your industry. Think about changes in consumption patterns that could decrease your market opportunity.

Look at this sample SWOT analysis in Figure 1.2, based on a small business (cupcake bakery). I will use the cupcake shop example a few times throughout the book to illustrate some of the tools and concepts. I chose the bakery because, well, who doesn't love cupcakes?

From the SWOT analysis, we can see that while the owners and employees are upbeat about the opportunity, there are real external threats from existing bakeries, as well as pricing pressure from grocery store cupcakes. A smart owner would want to aggressively explore their opportunities at the nearby business park to shore up its business.

You can see from this example the simple power this gives an organization to see its strengths, weaknesses, opportunities, and threats all in one place. It can help crystallize an organization's strategic direction and give leadership the direction they need to prioritize work and resources.

SWOT analysis does not need to be done only at the top level of the organization; it can be applied to all levels. In project and program management, SWOT analysis can be done by leaders of the project organization to help them see what they are doing well, and what their stakeholders need them to do better. SWOT analysis can identify areas

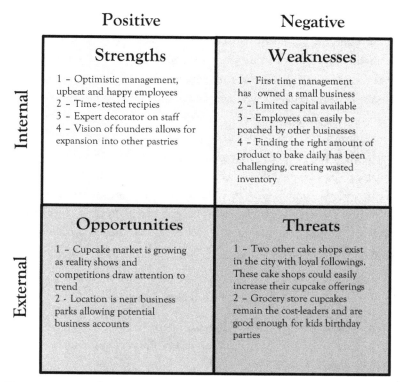

Figure 1.2 SWOT analysis—completed sample

where they need to bolster talent and areas where they can leverage their existing talent in new ways.

If you are assigned to a product launch project, you can use SWOT analysis to examine the product's potential in the designated market space. What are the product's strengths, weaknesses, opportunities, and threats? Answering these questions can help you find ways to build protective moats around your product and ensure better market positioning.

Application to Project and Program Management

Corporate strategy is arguably the most important function in an organization because the decisions and direction from this function profoundly affects the rest of the company. Understanding the basic concepts and tools used by corporate strategists is important to all aspiring leaders and should be of interest to project and program managers because understanding corporate strategy will help you understand why certain decisions are made. As project and program managers, we execute the corporate strategy. Additionally, when we are acting as portfolio managers, we can help to shape the strategic work an organization chooses to prioritize.

In this chapter, you were introduced to several strategic tools such as Porter's five forces, BCG matrix, and SWOT analysis that help inform your project and program management practice. SWOT analysis in particular can be done at the project and program level, as needed. It can help us with decision making by causing us to examine internal and external factors so that we can see potential next steps to take. This can be applicable for personal questions, career decisions, and as part of decision support work in our projects.

Additional Resources

Porter, M.E. March 1, 1979. "How Competitive Forces Shape Strategy." *Harvard Business*, https://hbr.org/1979/03/how-competitive-forces-shape-strategy.

Lidow, D. February 13, 2017. "A Better Way to Set Strategic Priorities." *Harvard Business*, https://hbr.org/2017/02/a-better-way-to-set-strategic-priorities.

CHAPTER 2

Economics and Decision Making

Why Study Economics

Economic principles undergird the decisions and strategies used by the largest international corporations and the smallest home businesses alike. Economic principles even help explain many of the mundane decisions we make in our lives. It's not just financial decisions. Economic principles apply to the way we use our time and the way we make decisions. It's all about trade-offs.

Economics has two primary branches. *Macroeconomics* studies broad economic impacts that affect global trade, government actions, and markets, including stock markets. Macroeconomic forces impact organizations and individuals as economies expand and contract. This is the branch most people think of when discussing economics. However, macroeconomic theory is less applicable to project and program managers because it is so broad. The problems we typically solve are different that those economists debate at the macro level.

Microeconomics, on the other hand, focuses on the behavior of individuals and organizations. Its theories and lessons are directly relevant to project and program management. Microeconomic theories are about working within constraints. Constraints of time, constraints of budget, constraints of choosing to do one thing at the expense of another. Sound like project management? Microeconomics describes why we choose to spend our time and money the way we do. Microeconomics will help us understand managing constraints.

This chapter will show the place of economics (specifically microeconomics) in project management. It will cover basic economic principles and introduce you to key tools for making better decisions.

Understanding the Basics

There are dozens, if not hundreds, of economic theories, and more are developed every year. However, there are a group foundational theories that are core to microeconomics and are good for project and program managers to know. As we review these theories together, think about their application to project and program management. I will call out ways I have seen these theories apply to our craft—but these theories are rich, and project and program management is complex—so I encourage you to find ways to apply them to your individual professional situations.

Scarcity

Scarcity may be the most fundamental concept in economics. The recognition that there is not enough time, money, or resources to satisfy all demands is at the core of economic theory. Economists study the behavior of people and organizations in making trade-off decisions related to scarcity. More than that, they have developed elaborate models and tools for helping people and organizations make those trade-off decisions.

Scarcity in Project and Program Management

Scarcity is at the heart of the project management triple constraint. Due to constraints on budget and time (and unlimited appetite for scope), a project is always constrained in a real (and an economic) sense.

The next time you are dealing with a budget, schedule, or scope issue, remind yourself that you are wrestling with a core economic principle! Project and program managers are, in a sense, economics practitioners. As we continue our review of economics principles, you will be introduced to some concepts that may help you as you wrestle with the natural scarcity problem built into every project.

Utility, Marginal Utility, and Marginal Cost

Utility refers to the amount of value a person or organization gets from consuming a resource. In plain language, it is how much satisfaction you get from something. Humans and organizations automatically seek to maximize the utility they receive in every transaction. Utility is defined this way:

Utility is a term in economics that refers to the total satisfaction received from consuming a good or service. Economic theories based on rational choice usually assume that consumers will strive to maximize their utility. The economic utility of a good or service is important to understand, because it directly influences the demand, and therefore price, of that good or service.[1]

It makes sense, then, that when people find consumption of a resource to be useful or enjoyable, they will want to consume it again. But the enjoyment of a second item may not be as useful as first. For example, the first French fry in a bag is a delight! The second, third, and even the 30th are probably going to be great. But what about the 100th fry? Or 1,000th fry? At some point, that warm, salty treat starts to taste more like cardboard than potato.

In weightier terms, this concept can apply to every important resource. The first barrel of oil consumed by a country is exceedingly valuable. But once all petroleum needs are met, those next barrels have decreased *marginal utility*. Marginal utility is the economic concept that each unit of a resource consumed may have a different value than the unit consumed before and the unit consumed after.

One of the great things about economics is that it is a social science that it is backed by math. Economists love graphs and often use them to explain concepts. In this chapter, we will honor the tradition of using simple graphs to explain economic concepts.

Let's look at the utility of consuming cupcakes (I told you in Chapter 1 you'd see more cupcake examples!). Figure 2.1 shows an imagined utility (benefit or pleasure) received after eating one cupcake (left side) and 20 cupcakes (right side) and all points in between. If you're like most people, the first cupcake will bring great pleasure. So will the second. But, as the number of cupcakes consumed increases, the pleasure (utility) decreases. Eventually, you will reach a point where consumption of the next cupcake reaches zero (it can also turn negative).

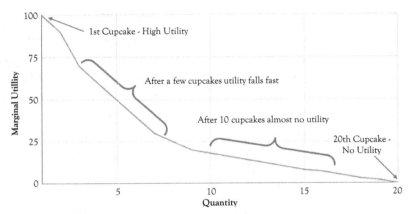

Figure 2.1 Marginal utility versus quantity

The concept of marginal utility can apply to project and program management. For example, one project update per month will provide great utility to your stakeholders. Increasing updates to weekly may also provide a good amount of benefit. But daily updates may become annoying. If we take it to extremes, a minute-by-minute update to stakeholders would likely provide negative benefit. Finding the right level of reporting is about maximizing the utility of the updates.

Another important consideration is that each additional unit consumed will have an additional cost. This is a supply-side concept related to the cost of producing one additional unit of any product. Similar to marginal utility, the cost of producing additional units can vary. For example, if a bakery running at full capacity can produce 10,000 cupcakes a month at an average of $1 per unit is asked to produce unit 10,001—the cost of that unit would be the cost of expanding the bakery. The shop owner is not likely to fulfill the request for cupcake 10,001 unless they believe that they can also sell the rest of the capacity available after the expansion (cupcakes 10,002 to 20,000).

Economic Utility for Project and Program Managers

- The application of utility is most easily demonstrated by the project resources available to any given project. For example, having one developer on a software project brings incredible marginal utility. Having two is likely better, but at some point, additional developers will bring no additional utility (or could negatively affect it if you have to manage their time even when they are not providing value). When you are looking at resourcing a project, you can help to justify your staffing requests in terms of utility (value) delivered by each requested resource and also call out that you are restraining from asking for more of a particular resource based on diminished utility.

- Additionally, as you think about adding resources, think about the marginal costs. In some technical projects, data center space is required to be purchased by the *rack*. The cost to add capacity within a rack can be relatively inexpensive—but once you go beyond the space within a rack, you must pay for an all new rack even if you only use one small portion of the new rack. The marginal cost to add capacity within the original rack is constant—but once you go beyond that rack, the marginal cost can jump.

Opportunity Costs

Opportunity cost is simple to understand. When a choice is made to take an action, there is also another choice made: the action that will *not* be taken. Opportunity cost is the value of what was given up when the choice was made. This economic principle is so fundamental to project management professionals that it is part of some program management certification exams. The definition of opportunity cost, per the Cambridge Dictionary, is "the value of the option you do not choose, when choosing between two possible options.[2]"

A simple example of opportunity cost is related to the reading of this book. The opportunity cost of reading this book is whatever you would have done instead. Maybe you would have turned on the television and watched your favorite program. Or maybe it was getting to bed early. Whatever the trade-off, you instead chose to learn key business principles that will improve your project management skills (good choice!).

Like most economic theories, opportunity cost is easy to calculate and graph. The formula is simple:

$$\frac{\text{Value of What's Lost}}{\text{Value of What's Gained}}$$

Here is a simple example: You make $50k per year as a project manager. You got an offer from another company where you would make $55k—but you are really happy where you are. You decide to stay in your current role. Here is the opportunity cost:

$$\frac{\$5,000 \text{ (amount lost by not taking the job)}}{\$50,000 \text{ (current salary)}}$$

This makes your opportunity cost $0.10, meaning that for every dollar you earn at your current job, you could have made $0.10 more at the other job.

Let's look at a more complex example: As the Covid-19 pandemic was starting to spread, several companies made announcements about shifting their production to build much-needed ventilators. However, this meant that those companies would not be manufacturing their normal goods. Let's look at what an opportunity cost analysis might have looked like for a fictional company.

Assumptions: A medical device company specializing in making heart monitors can produce 12 devices a day and charge $60k per unit. They estimate that they can manufacture ventilators on the same production line—but they can only produce six per day. They estimate they can charge $100k per ventilator. The data is outlined in Table 2.1.

The production trade-offs would look like Figure 2.2.

Table 2.1 Opportunity cost example

	Cost per unit	Units per day	Potential income
Heart machine	$60,000	12	$720,000
Ventilator	$100,000	6	$600,000

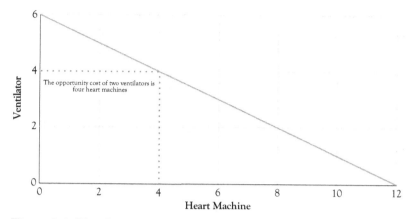

Figure 2.2 Ventilator versus heart machine

Recalling that the calculation for opportunity cost is the value of what is lost over what is gained, the opportunity cost for the company to build two ventilators per day would be four heart machines:

$$\frac{\$240{,}000 \text{ (four heart machines)}}{\$200{,}000 \text{ (two ventilators)}}$$

Thus, the opportunity cost to build two ventilators is $40,000 (technically it is $1.20, meaning a loss of $0.20 per dollar if the company builds ventilators instead of heart machines). If a company were making a strictly financial decision, they would not change production to ventilators. A company may still choose to make them despite the financial analysis if leadership has a passion for helping people, they can get positive publicity, they can get a tax break, or many other reasons that make sense to leadership.

Opportunity Cost for Project and Program Managers

Early career project and program managers often have projects assigned to them by management with little input on what they are assigned. More senior professionals can sometimes influence the work they are able to do. At the top of the chain, if you are working at the portfolio level, you may be involved in decisions on what projects get funded and which one's do not. You might even be involved in developing cost estimates and trade-off analyses. Opportunity cost analysis becomes very important at that level of our profession.

It is a common practice in portfolio management to stack rank projects by priority and then draw a line at what is funded (above the line) and not funded (below the line). This exercise is all about opportunity costs. Those below the line are the opportunity cost of doing the projects above the line.

Linegate

While running the Business Technology (BT) Project Management Office (PMO) at a prominent cloud company, my team and I initiated the company's first-ever cross-functional portfolio prioritization process. We were developing BT's proposed annual budget, and we had reserved several million dollars for technology projects requested by our internal business partners. In prior years, BT leadership would decide what projects we would fund on behalf of our business partners. This year we wanted to mature our process and involve our partners in budget decisions because they are closest to the work that needs to be done, and we believed better decisions would be made.

Preparation for the first meeting took months. On the day of the meeting, we had more than 90 8.5 × 11 printed sheets representing each project vying for the available budget taped to one large wall. The combined ask of those projects was roughly three times the available budget. We knew it was going to be a challenging meeting. We had vice presidents from all of our primary business partners packed into a room for eight hours. We started the prioritization discussions, and as projects moved up and down in priority, we moved a piece of blue tape around to show *the line* between funded and unfunded projects. Near the end of the meeting, the conversations become more complex, and we abandoned the tape—always keeping the new virtual line carefully communicated.

By the end of the meeting, we were exhausted, but we'd completed our mission and had a prioritized list of projects above and below the line. However, a problem developed soon after the meeting when one particularly difficult business partner started to dispute our resulting list. It turns out the partner took pictures of the wall at the end of the meeting, including the placement of the tape. When he compared my finalized list with his pictures showing the location of the blue tape, he started to pound us with complaints that some of his *critical* projects were below the line on my list when the tape on the wall showed otherwise. It is hard to argue with pictures, but the rest of the attendees all understood where the line was, so we stood by our final conclusions. This incident was dubbed *linegate* by the team, and in future meetings, we were even more careful when talking about *the line*.

Another common issue project and program managers can face is deciding the best option between multiple design solutions. This is a type of opportunity cost decision. It is common for projects to have multiple viable solution options—and not all solutions have the same features. Scorecards and other analyses can help highlight the trade-offs of each solution. If you are tasked with running an analysis like this, remember that this is a common opportunity cost problem.

Supply and Demand

When people think about economics, they often think about supply and demand—it's almost a cliché—but understanding the interaction between supply and demand is important. First, some definitions:

Demand: Demand is an economic principle referring to a consumer's desire to purchase goods and services and a willingness to pay a price for a specific good or service. Holding all other factors constant, an increase in the price of a good or service will decrease the quantity demanded and vice versa.[3]

Supply: Supply is a fundamental economic concept that describes the total amount of a specific good or service that is available to consumers. Supply can relate to the amount available at a specific price or the amount available across a range of prices if displayed on a graph.[4]

When we talk supply and demand, it is essential to understand two additional definitions:

Substitute Goods: A substitute, or substitutable good, in economics and consumer theory refers to a product or service that consumers see as essentially the same or similar-enough to another product. Put simply, a substitute is a good that can be used in place of another.[5]

Complementary Goods: A complementary good or service is an item used in conjunction with another good or service. Usually, the complementary good has little to no value when consumed alone, but when combined with another good or service, it adds to the overall value of the offering. A product can be considered a complement when it shares a beneficial relationship with another product offering, for example, an iPhone and the apps used with it.[6]

Now that we understand the basic definitions, let's examine the forces at work. As with all things economic, it's typical to look at these forces in graph form. Note that quantity is on the x-axis on the bottom, and price is on the vertical y-axis. Demand lines start high and head down as quantity increase. Supply lines are the opposite. They start low and go higher as prices increase.

In Figure 2.3, let's imagine you want to start a cupcake business. You've been doing some research and learned that people seem willing to pay between $2 and $7 per cupcake. You estimate that you will barely break even at $2, so you want to charge as much as possible. The upward sloping supply line represents the number of cupcakes you're willing to bake at each price level. The downward sloping demand line represents the number of cupcakes you believe people will be willing to buy at each price level. As expected, the less you charge, the greater the demand, and the more you charge, the less demand exists.

The point at which the lines intersect is where quantity demanded is equal to quantity delivered—it's the equilibrium point (about $4 on our graph). To ensure you sell all the cupcakes you produce, and to maximize your profit, you will want to charge the equilibrium price. If you price higher than equilibrium, you will need to bake less cupcakes or risk some

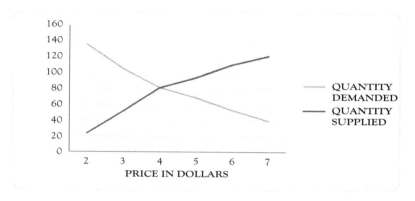

Figure 2.3 Quantity demanded and quantity supplied

going to waste. If you charge less than equilibrium, you will be losing revenue you could otherwise capture.

As interesting as this might be, there is a lot more we can learn from supply and demand graphs. For example, what would happen to the preceding graph if a new fad diet swept the nation offering (likely dubious) evidence that eating cupcakes will help you look younger and live longer. The demand line (downward sloping) would jump up. Look at Figure 2.4.

The increased demand gives us a new equilibrium point of about $6 per cupcake, and the number of units you can sell at that price is much higher, thanks to the new fad. The same thing can happen to the supply

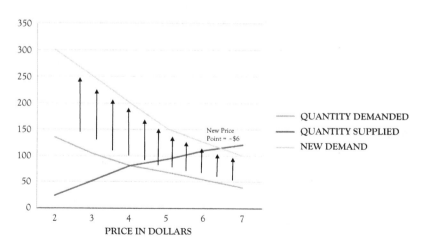

Figure 2.4 New demand curve

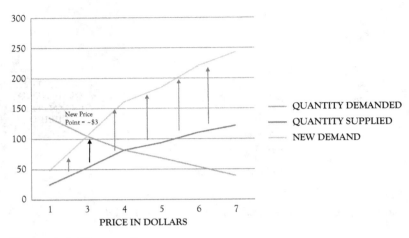

Figure 2.5 New supply curve

curve on the graph. If the market were suddenly flooded with cupcakes, the equation would change again. Starting with the original graph, Figure 2.5 shows the results: The result of the increased supply would put pressure on what you would be able to charge. There are too many cup-cakes for people to pay $4. The new equilibrium price would be about $3.

Now that you understand the basics of supply and demand, it is important talk about substitution and complementary goods because of their impact on supply and demand. It is conceivable that as prices for cupcakes go up, goods similar to cupcakes would also see an increased demand. Brownies and other pastries could see a halo effect from the cupcake diet, keeping cupcake prices more in check. Similarly, comple-mentary effects could cause things like milk to see an increase in demand as cupcakes are consumed more frequently.

Supply and Demand for Project and Program Managers

One of the applications of supply and demand of greatest interest to project and program managers has nothing to do with how we manage project work and everything to do with our overall career prospects. I'm talking about the demand for project management in the economy and the supply of qualified project managers available. Our livelihoods are subject to the laws of supply and demand. If the demand for project and program managers were to spike, the demand curve would jump, causing the point of equilibrium with supply to drive up what we should (theoretically) be paid. Unfortunately, the opposite is true. If the number of project managers were to surge, the supply curve would jump, and the salary we can demand would go down.

Of the two scenarios, I pay most attention to the supply of project management professionals available. Given that project management has a solid career path with good compensation, it draws a lot of people into the profession each year. On top of that, the Project Management Institute (PMI) issued a report in 2017 predicting that over the next 10 years, the demand for project managers would outstrip demand for other types of workers.[7] They estimated 22 million new project management jobs through 2027. The expected demand remains solid. My concern is that as demand increases, it will cause a rush of underqualified *project managers* who could dilute the value of the profession. I also worry that the proliferation of agile and project certifications will create a *diploma mill* dynamic. However, because the demand still remains strong, my concerns about the project manager supply curve jumping up are so far unfounded.

Decision Making for Project and Program Managers

MBA students are taught multiple decision-making techniques while matriculating through core and elective classes. Some are taught through a financial lens, some through a human resource lens, some through an economic lens, and so on. For the remainder of this chapter, I will introduce you to three decision-making techniques that can be applied to various problems a project or program manager is likely to see at some point in their career. These decision-making techniques are not exclusive to economics. In fact, these are often taught in other classes, but I have gathered them together in one place for convenience.

Decisions can be classified in many ways, but I have found that most can be sorted into two general buckets: strategic or tactical. In my career, I have found project and program managers are typically in a decision support role rather than functioning as decision makers, especially with strategic decisions.

- *Strategic decisions* change the direction or focus of an organization, team, or project. As discussed in Chapter 1, these are typically complex decisions with multiple variables and may be influenced by external (marketplace) dynamics. Generally speaking, project and program managers are not asked to make these kinds of decisions, but we are often asked to gather data that can influence these decisions. When operating at a portfolio level, influence on strategic direction becomes much stronger, and depending on the structure of an organization, a portfolio leader can wield great influence on strategy.

- *Tactical decisions* are typically made at lower levels of an organization, including at the project and program level. These are the decisions that take place in support of the broader strategic decision. For example, a company decides it needs to improve the ability of its employees to work productively and securely from home. That strategic direction describes *what* the company will do. Project managers may lead initiatives to decide *how* solutions should be deployed, the sequence of deployment, and *which* employees receive new capabilities first.

Decision Tree Analysis

Decision trees model the possible outcomes accompanied by the estimated likelihood of occurrence, which is a powerful way to map a real-world decision. Decision trees can be as simple or complex as needed for the situation.

Decision tree analysis first appeared several decades ago, and it has been a staple in MBA education ever since. I am a little surprised at how long decision trees have existed because I had never heard of the technique during my first 10 years of corporate experience. It's a shame it is not used more often in business. It can be a powerful but simple tool for cutting through the noise involved in complex decisions. I will show the basics of the technique by using a scenario that may be familiar to some project and program managers. Note that decision trees can be very complex, and there is specialized software available to help with the more complex decisions.

Decision trees are excellent for developing probability-based scenarios. With the right information, we can apply the probabilities and estimates to develop the fiscal impact of each option.

Example: Throwing Water on Our Product Launch

For this example, imagine you are managing the launch of a new all-electric all-terrain vehicle (ATV). This is the first all-electric ATV produced by your company and the first of its kind in the marketplace. Dealers and customers have been excitedly waiting for this new product for some time. Vehicle details have been leaked and the press and potential buyers are excited to learn more.

The CEO wants to do the official launch of the product in the great outdoors, where the vehicle's capabilities can be showcased. A location in a popular recreation park has been secured, and you are now 10 days from the launch. You were made aware that a competitor is planning the launch of their electric ATV in the next few months and is planning a big outdoor demonstration of the vehicle. Rumors are that they are considering an early launch so that they can claim to be the first to market. Due to this competitive threat, delay is not an option. It was estimated that the value of a successful launch is $10M to your company.

You are working hard to ensure the launch will be successful when you learn that weather forecasters are predicting a 30 percent chance of a major storm hitting in the area of the recreation park on the day of the launch, potentially reducing the value of the launch to $2M to the company because many media outlets are likely to skip the event (and you could not show off the vehicles full capability in the rain). Senior leaders ask you what you are going to do in the event of rain. You are a professional, so you have a backup plan to do the launch in an indoor conference center—but the launch will not have as much impact because the press will not be able to see the vehicles in action. You estimate the value of the indoor launch to be $6M. If you are going to use the conference center, you will have to make the decision to shift to that location at least seven days prior to the launch so that invitations to the press can be modified and preparations made in the backup location.

Management asks you for a decision. What are you going to do?

Decision trees are composed of decision points (shown with squares) and chance events (shown with circles). The options are all branches along the tree. We will use a concept called expected value—essentially multiplying the likelihood of an event by the economic value—to determine the best economic choice for the project manager to make. Figure 2.6 shows the sample decision tree.

By taking the combined expected value of the decision to do the launch outdoors, we are able to calculate an expected value of $7.6M, which is slightly higher than the expected value of an indoor launch ($6M). Thus, you can present to management that your assessment is the company should move forward with its original plan but knowing there is a risk of value destruction if the rain does hit. A more conservative company may choose to do the launch indoors and get a more-sure $6M benefit—but at least you can see the value a decision tree can bring to a difficult decision.

Of course, this is a simplified decision tree for illustrative purposes. When decisions get complicated, it can help to map out the potential options. Within the project management realm, there are a number of decisions that lend themselves well to decision tree analysis. Decisions around vendor selection (inexperienced but cheap versus experienced but costly), feature decisions, and even project selection can all benefit from decision tree analysis.

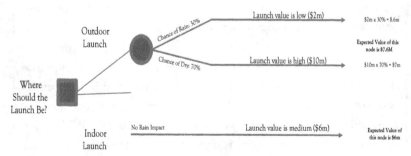

Figure 2.6 Example decision tree for ATV launch location

Decision Matrix

Like decision trees, decision matrixes are great for strategic decisions, but because they are a little simpler to put together and interpret, they can also be used for tactical decisions.

Decision matrixes are great for making decisions with multiple variables. These are the complex kind of decisions that we often come up against in project management (and in life). Some examples of decisions that lend themselves to a decision matrix are:

- Location choices (deciding between new office locations)
- Deciding between two vendors
- Hiring decisions between a group of candidates bringing different skillsets and experiences
- Just about any time you are deciding between multiple choices with several variables

Decision matrixes are popular because they are created in a familiar table format. The alternatives are typically listed across the top (column headers), and the criteria are listed down the left-hand side as the first cell in each row. This allows each alternative to be summarized at the bottom. Of course, as these are in a tabular format, you could switch the alternatives and criteria, but then the table summary will be on the right side. Matrixes are best for decisions requiring more than two alternatives, but not more than eight or ten alternatives because they can become unwieldy.

Figure 2.7 illustrates a sample decision matrix for an enterprise e-mail productivity tool recommendation for your organization.

The example in Figure 2.7 is simple, and the math is a straight-line calculation. It shows that, with all criteria of equal value, Microsoft (MS) Office 365 and Google Suite are the top contenders. But what happens if the criteria are not equally valued by your company? What if the company valued cost and customization the most? This tool allows for weighting of criteria such that the most important criteria are valued the most. Look at the updated matrix with simple weightings (one, two, or three, with three being the most important). The company's relative weightings change the analysis substantially, as can be seen in Figure 2.8.

Alternatives

	MS Office 365	Google Suite	LibreOffice	Paper, Pencil, and Carrier Pigeon
E-mail ability	10	10	5	0
Presentation ability	10	8	6	3
Spreadsheet ability	10	8	6	3
Ease of Collaboration	8	10	5	2
Customization	3	2	3	10
Security	8	8	8	4
Annual Cost	3	5	7	10
Employee familiarity	9	8	3	8
Compatibility	8	8	5	1
	69	67	48	41

Criteria

Summary Scores
(Non-weighted)

Figure 2.7 Example decision matrix for productivity tools

If the company values customization and cost above all else, the results become a lot more interesting. Weighting is powerful, but if used wrong, it could create some interesting results. Imagine recommending paper, pencil, and carrier pigeon as viable alternatives to Microsoft or Google!

Alternatives

	Weighting	MS Office 365	Google Suite	LibreOffice	Paper, Pencil, and Carrier Pigeon
E-mail ability	1	10	10	5	0
Presentation ability	1	10	8	6	3
Spreadsheet ability	1	10	8	6	3
Ease of Collaboration	1	8	10	5	2
Customization	3	9	6	9	30
Security	1	8	8	8	4
Annual Cost	3	9	15	21	30
Employee familiarity	1	9	8	3	8
Compatibility	1	8	8	5	1
		81	81	68	81

Criteria

Weighting: The company
values customization and
cost above all else

Summary Scores
(Non-weighted)

Figure 2.8 Example weighted decision matrix for productivity tools

The decision matrix is one of the most versatile of the decision-making tools. It is appealing because it is easy to understand. Leaders are able to consume the results and see numeric comparisons. The trick with them is getting the content of the cells filled with the right information. Deciding on weighting is also quite tricky if you use it. It requires talking to stakeholders to gauge the relative importance of each criteria. You may hear conflicting opinions from leadership, and when you publish the results, it is possible people will want to question and change the weighting so that the results more closely reflect the results they expected.

As stated earlier in this section, you can create a decision matrix for many decisions you're likely to be involved in as a project and program manager. On a personal level, they are great to use for decisions around potential job offers; you can weight the aspects of the jobs and offers that are of most value to you.

You can also use a decision matrix to help you decide what business school you should choose to pursue an MBA, if you decide to do it. List out the options on the top, and the criteria down the side. It would help you clarify your thinking. There are many great resources online, including templates, that can help you build your first decision matrix.

Pareto Analysis

Pareto analysis may already be part of your project management toolkit. It has been part of some project management certification curricula for many years because it is a powerful tool to narrow down the most important things to focus on. It is also based on a very common rule of thumb that most people intuitively understand: the 80/20 rule.[8]

The 80/20 rule can be applied in a positive or negative manner. The positive side of the rule says that 80 percent of a benefit can be derived from 20 percent of the effort. The flip side says that 80 percent of the problem is caused by 20 percent of the issues. A Pareto analysis can help us as project and program managers to focus on those 20 percent of items that matter the most.

Vilfredo Pareto (1848–1923) was an Italian economist (and philosopher, sociologist, and engineer) who first observed that, in general, 80 percent of the wealth of a nation is controlled by 20 percent of the population. This observation was used by others to extend this principle and create the analysis that is today named after Pareto.

A Pareto analysis is a systematic discovery of the (few) factors that have the most impact. A Pareto analysis can powerfully cut through a lot of data to find the pieces that are the most important to focus on as a project team.

A Pareto analysis can be done in any common spreadsheet application. Traditionally, they are vertical bar charts. To create a Pareto analysis, you will need a list of the causes or defects you are seeing, sorted into buckets by type. For example, if you are trying to determine why a customer service team is always behind on its cases, you can sort all of the cases it receives into issue types such as installation issues, application crashes, incompatibilities, user error, feature requests, and so on.

Once you have the appropriate data, create a vertical bar chart with the grouped causes along the bottom (x-axis). The y-axis is the count of each issue type, sorted with the highest counts on the left, descending to the right. Look at Figure 2.9, a sample Pareto analysis for the problem described.

If you were assigned to manage a project related to improving customer service, the kind of analysis in our sample Pareto chart would give you real direction on where to put your efforts. Focusing on improving

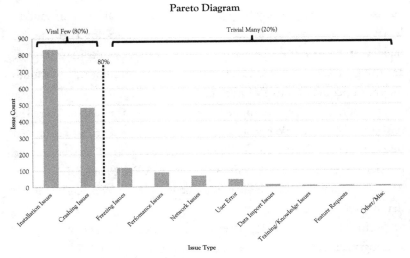

Figure 2.9 Sample pareto analysis

installation processes would greatly reduce calls to customer service as would development efforts to stabilize the application (stop the crashing).

Application to Project and Program Managers

The study of economics has applications to many aspects of our personal and professional lives. In this chapter, I showed that project managers wrestle with economic trade-offs regularly as the they manage the triple constraint of schedule, budget, and scope. Additionally, understanding and embracing the concepts of utility, and supply and demand can elevate our project management practices.

Finally, we examined three powerful decision-making tools that can be directly applied to the kinds of challenges we face in our projects. Decision trees, decision matrixes, and Pareto analyses can elevate decision making within our projects, and even the perception of leadership about your skills as a project and program manager.

Additional Resources

The concepts and decision tools taught in this chapter can be complex—especially when you attempt to use them the first time. I am including a list of resources that may be of help to you as you apply these in your own project management practice. There are several free textbooks that can supplement your learning (try open.umn.edu).

Other Resources:

- Decision trees: https://hbr.org/1964/07/decision-trees-for-decision-making
- Decision matrix: https://asq.org/quality-resources/decision-matrix
- Pareto analysis: https://asq.org/quality-resources/pareto
- Investopedia.com has great, simple definitions and examples for most financial and economic terms and concepts

CHAPTER 3

Corporate Finance

Why Study Finance?

Unless you work for a government agency or a non-profit, the organization you work for will have at least one owner, or several (called shareholders), who invested in the company and expect a return on their investment. Even government agencies and non-profits have to manage budgets and use their funds responsibly. Finance is all about the fiscal structure of an organization and how the organization receives, invests, and spends its funds. It is closely aligned to accounting, but differs from it in that accounting is about the tracking and reporting of where funds have been spent. Accounting is a financial reporting language and practice. Finance is about ensuring the financial stability of an organization such that it can operate effectively and build stakeholder value (also called equity).

I consider a basic understanding of finance absolutely critical for project and program managers in two ways. First, there is a practical value to it. You may be called on to work with a finance partner on your project budgeting. Understanding financial basics such as capital versus expense is foundational in those conversations. It is also critical to understand key finance dates such as month-end, quarter-end, and year-end. If you have a budget item that is slipping by a month, it may not be a big deal if it slips within the confines of a quarter—but you may have a huge problem if it goes past a fiscal quarter or year-end boundary. You may see a budget as a list of items you need to spend money on as you execute your project. Your finance partner sees the same list spread across months in smaller pieces and in buckets you may not recognize. Sometimes this happens in the background, sometimes you need to get involved.

As you move up to portfolio management, you may be called on to do more extensive budgeting and investment evaluation. Having a solid grasp of basic finance will be critical to you at that point in your career.

The second critical reason to understand finance is so that you can see how the work you're doing is tied to the greater organizational picture. Organizations only take on projects they believe will benefit them more than if they put the money in the bank (or the stock market) and collected the returns. So, the fact that you are managing a project means there is an investment expectation (even if it's not actually calculated) for that project. Further, when a company reports its earnings to the Securities and Exchange Commission (if it is public), the work you are doing is bundled into those numbers. It can be eye opening to see where your project work is represented in these reports.

In this chapter, we will explore the basics of finance as well as introduce you to several financial analyses that you may be asked to calculate at some point in your career. Please note that finance and accounting are two sides of the same coin—but they are not the same. The next chapter will dive into the world of accounting. As we discuss finance in this chapter, you may wonder why I am not discussing certain principles. The answer may be that I felt it belongs more in the accounting chapter than this one. This chapter and the next are packed with fundamental concepts and very useful tools. We cover in these chapters what professionals spend years studying—so I recommend you review the *Additional Resources* section at the end of this chapter so that you can continue your studies of these concepts.

If you are working for an organization that does not report its finances publicly, there are still many great reasons to become familiar with finance. As you will learn in the next section, there are a few core financial reports that all publicly traded organizations (and many private and not-for-profits) use to measure their financial health. These financial reports are a major component in stock market valuations of companies. So, even if you don't need this information right now in your career, there are other places it's applicable, and it could make you a smarter investor.

Understanding the Basics

Finance is a complex field that requires a lot of specialized knowledge before you can work in it. The good news is that we as project and program managers don't need to understand all aspects of finance, but there are several core concepts that we should definitely understand.

The Fiscal Calendar

One of the most basic terms that you will hear in most organizations is *fiscal* year. This year may or may not be the same as a calendar year. It marks the annual period the company observes. A definition of fiscal year is as follows:

> *A period of twelve months (not always January 1st to December 31st) for which a government or business plans its management of money.*[1]

Why would a company choose to have a fiscal year different from a normal calendar year? Due to its typical business cycle. For example, retail stores do the vast majority of their business the last six weeks of the calendar year, so they often have a fiscal year that ends on January 31. This gives them time to close the accounting books and prepare their financial statements. This means their fiscal year would start on February 1. The first day of an organization's fiscal year has nothing to do with the first day they started business.

This matters to project and program managers because our project dates are often tied to quarter start and end dates. Budgets are often bucketed into quarters, so project funding may become available at the start of the quarter (and may disappear at the end of the quarter if not spent). Additionally, it is common for the start of each fiscal year to usher in a rush of new project starts (and the end of the year to cause a rush to finish projects). Annual planning processes can also create a flurry of work for project and program managers as management tries to understand the amount of work departments want to take on in the coming year.

If you manage projects for a finance department, or if you have members of a finance team on your project, you will need to pay attention to *blackout dates* where finance professionals focus exclusively on month, quarter, or annual closing of books. These can last for a few days or a few weeks, depending on the close period. As you plan your projects, you will have to account for these dates in your schedule or it will slip when the finance team disappears to close the books.

Public Versus Private Companies

I have worked for both private and public companies. Each has its advantages and disadvantages. Public companies have easier access to capital (funding) and are generally more visible. This comes at the cost of administrative and regulatory overhead. Private companies have more flexibility in the way they operate and have less overhead. As long as the investors (owners) are happy, the company can invest in what it wants. However, should the company need additional investment to grow, it could be challenged to find additional funding. Most investors want to know when they can get their investment back—and private companies don't have a good story around that unless they are planning on going public. Either way, it is important to understand what kind of organization you work for because it impacts many aspects of your experience as an employee.

Financial Forecasting

While helping manage a $150M department portfolio, I became very familiar with the challenges of doing financial forecasts. While the actual forecasting was done by our finance partner, we would regularly work to better predict the expenses of the department. No matter how hard we

---

Going Public

Early in my career, I worked for a start-up company that was attempting to go public. As a private firm, it was hard for leadership to raise money. A lot of time was spent contacting potential investors and convincing them the company had a bright future. I was involved in developing parts of the registration statement (part of the requirement to file an IPO). It was eye opening to a non-finance professional how much documentation and effort had to go into this statement. But the effort was worth it to the founder because getting access to public markets was important to the company's long-term viability.

Eventually, the company chose not to go public and, instead, sold itself to another firm. This sale provided what the original investors really wanted, which was a way to get their investment back. The new owners decided to take the technology owned by the firm and leave all the rest, meaning the employees—myself included—were out of a job, and all of the stock options I'd been given were instantly worthless.

Being aware of the implications of public versus private is important as you make your career decisions.

tried, it seemed there were always variances from our forecast compared to what we actually spent. Being able to accurately forecast expenses (and revenue!) is very important to publicly traded companies that must signal to financial markets their best financial forecasts. If a department is off in their forecast versus actuals, it can cause problems for leadership.

One of the most surprising things for me was that running under forecast was just as big of a problem as running over budget. Budget managers should be especially concerned because if they significantly underspend, they are likely to have their budgets cut going forward. There is also an opportunity cost to the organization because the funds could have been deployed elsewhere to build the business.

As project and program managers, we may be asked to provide guidance on how close our project spend is tracking to our budget, so being honest and realistic (not padding), our budgets will assist the broader organization and is a best practice.

Time Value of Money

A dollar today is more valuable than a dollar a year from now. This is the *time value* of money, and it's a basic principle in finance. Think about it. Not only are the forces of inflation eroding the value of the dollar across the year, but you could have put that dollar to work immediately earning interest in an investment. Many of the tools used in financial analysis incorporate this principle.

I introduce this concept to you for two reasons. First is for personal enrichment as you think about your individual financial investments; it's important to recognize that any money that is not working for you is losing value. It can also guide decisions where payment can be delayed. Companies routinely delay commercial payments to the very end of the agreed terms (and sometimes a little longer) in recognition of this principal (and as part of a cash management strategy). Whether you do this in your own life is, of course, up to you.

The second reason I introduced this concept is because there are real-world tools and analyses used in corporate finance where the time value of money undergirds the entire calculation. Later in this chapter, we will look at several financial tools, a few of which are directly related to this concept.

Financial Reports

When you hear the term *financial report*, you may be thinking of any spreadsheet where numbers are analyzed or reported. While this is technically correct, this section will explore three very specific financial reports that, when taken together, give you a complete look at the financial health of the reporting organization. For publicly traded companies, these three statements must be issued each quarter. You will be familiar with some of these, but you may not understand the interplay between them because they are all connected.

Publishing regular financial reports is legally required of public companies. These reports are scrutinized by investment analysts, government entities, and individual investors alike. Even if you don't have a lot of interaction with organization finance teams, learning the basics of these reports could make you a smarter personal investor. Some basic definitions are as follows:

Balance Sheet: The balance sheet is fundamental to understanding how much money an organization has and how much debt it owes. It reports on the assets, liabilities, and shareholder equity of the organization. Together these numbers paint a picture of the overall health of a company at a single point in time (the as-of date of the balance sheet).[2]

Asset: An asset is anything of value or a resource of value that can be converted into cash. Individuals, companies, and governments own assets. For a company, an asset might generate revenue, or a company might benefit in some way from owning or using the asset.[3]

Liability: A liability is something a person or company owes, usually a sum of money. Liabilities are settled over time through the transfer of economic benefits including money, goods, or services.[4]

Equity: Equity, typically referred to as shareholders' equity (or owners' equity' for privately held companies), represents the amount of money that would be returned to a company's shareholders if all of the assets were liquidated and all of the company's debt was paid off.[5]

The structure of balance sheets is consistent and supports this fundamental equation: Assets = Liabilities + Shareholder Equity. True to its name, the right- and left-hand sides of the balance sheet have to balance, per the equation. The left-hand side is always the assets of the company. These assets can include cash, cash equivalents (treasury bills, short-term government bonds, and other ultra-safe investments), real estate, inventory, and receivables. It can also contain other items such as goodwill and intangible assets that are a little esoteric, so we won't discuss in this book. These assets are totaled at the bottom.

On the right-hand side in a list in the organization's liabilities. Liabilities are anything the company owes and can even include elements for risk. Common liabilities include accounts payable (purchases the company has made but not paid for yet), short-term debts, long-term debts, and a few other items that project and program managers are not likely to run across. These liabilities are totaled at the bottom.

Below liabilities is another section that is often called shareholder equity, total shareholder equity, or just equity. This section reports assets, minus liabilities, and represents the value that the organization has created for shareholders. This is really basic, but I believe is worth repeating: Shareholder equity is what is left after all liabilities are subtracted from all assets. If you think about a small single-owner business, this would be what the value of the business is to the owner.

Let's take a look at the basic balance sheet structure in Table 3.1.

Table 3.1 Balance sheet structure

Assets	Liabilities
Cash	Accounts payable
Marketable securities	Accrued liabilities
Prepaid expenses	Customer prepayments
Accounts receivable	Taxes payable
Inventory	Short-term debt
Fixed assets	Long-term debt
Less: accumulated depreciation	**Shareholder equity**
	Stock
	Additional paid-in capital
	Retained earnings
Assets = Liabilities + Stakeholder equity	
Assets − Liabilities = Stakeholder equity	

I added the equations on the bottom to remind us of the mathematical relationship between each part of the balance sheet. The left and the right always balance.

Think about the implications for shareholders. As assets increase (good) or liabilities decrease (good), the amount of shareholder equity gets proportionally larger, increasing the value to shareholders. As assets decrease (bad) or liabilities increase (bad) the amount of shareholder equity decreases, lowering the value to shareholders.

An important consideration for project and program managers is the impact of the projects they're working on to an organization's balance sheet. For projects that are *capital* projects, much or all of the cost of the project moves from the *cash* line of the asset side, to the *fixed assets* line on the same side. The net impact of the project is neutral to the balance sheet short term. Over time, the *fixed assets* are depreciated and leave the asset side, lowering the *shareholder equity*. This should be offset, however, by benefits derived by doing the project (new business, better efficiency, etc.).

If your project is not a capital project and is burning cash (salaries, vendor fees, subscriptions), this is likely coming out of the *cash* line within *assets* and leaving the balance sheet, shrinking *shareholder equity*. This is not as bad as it sounds, and many companies prefer to simply expense their projects.

As previously stated, the balance sheet is only one of three important financial reports. As we examine the other financial reports, we will refer back to the interaction the report has to the balance sheet.

Income Statement

The income statement shows an organization's profit or loss for a period of time. It shows revenue that came in and expenditures that went out over the period, which is different than the balance sheet, which shows the total value of an organization at a single point in time. Income statements show multiple profitability calculations such as operating profit, pre-tax profit, and after-tax profitability. We will not cover the differences in this book, but there are many great resources online if you are interested in learning more.

To really understand the income statement, we need to be clear on some definitions. First revenue:

Revenue: Revenue is the income generated from normal business operations and includes discounts and deductions for returned merchandise. It is the top line or gross income figure from which costs are subtracted to determine net income.[6]

Revenue can include sales of product and an sales of services. Revenue does not include the costs to build or acquire the products or services you sell. For public companies, there are extensive rules around when revenue can actually be recognized (meaning when it can show up on the income statement).

Now let's define expenses:

Expenses: An expense is the cost of operations that a company incurs to generate revenue. As the popular saying goes, "it costs money to make money." Common expenses include payments to suppliers, employee wages, factory leases, and equipment depreciation.[7]

Expenses are the costs to the organization to run the business. In most organizations, employee salaries are the biggest expense. Other common expenses are related to the costs of goods sold (manufacturing costs), lease or rental costs, equipment costs, and so on. The rules around expenses are complex but important. Whether a project is classified as *capital* or *expense matters* for the depreciation line within expense section of the income statement. If you have a capital project, it will be *put in service* at some point, which means accounting will start to depreciate the costs over time.

Additionally, I have been in organizations where managing accruals is important. Accruals are a necessary part of the expense section and are for identifying costs that a company has incurred, but for which it has not yet been billed. An important accounting principle is to tie costs as closely as possible to the time they are incurred. In Chapter 4, *Corporate Accounting,* I will provide additional details about accruals.

To continue, we need to understand other key parts of an income statement:

Net income: Net income (NI), also called net earnings, is calculated as sales minus cost of goods sold (COGS), selling, general and administrative expenses, operating expenses, depreciation, interest, taxes, and other expenses. It is a useful number for investors to assess how much revenue exceeds the expenses of an organization. This number appears on a company's income statement and is also an indicator of a company's profitability.[8]

Gross profit: Gross profit is the profit a company makes after deducting the costs associated with making and selling its products, or the costs associated with providing its services. Gross profit will appear on a company's income statement and can be calculated by subtracting the cost of goods sold (COGS) from revenue (sales). These figures can be found on a company's income statement. Gross profit may also be referred to as sales profit or gross income.[9]

After-tax profit: After-tax profit is the bottom-line calculation that includes all revenue and expenses, including federal and state taxes (if applicable). This is what the organization made in profit during the year after accounting for all revenue and expenses.

The income statement tells us how profitable the organization was during a defined time period. When combined with the balance sheet, it starts to tell a powerful story about the organization. Knowing how to read an income statement is part of basic financial literacy, and I recommend you take time to gain proficiency in this area.

Cash Flow Statement

Now that we understand balance sheets and income statements, it's important to understand the concept of cash flow. This particular report is more complicated to understand but is absolutely vital to the health of an organization.

To understand cash flow, it is important to understand that the revenue side of an income statement does not necessarily show the amount of cash that came into the business for the period. Here is a definition of cash flow statement:

The statement of cash flows, or the cash flow statement, is a finan-
cial statement that summarizes the amount of cash and cash equiva-
lents entering and leaving a company.

The cash flow statement (CFS) measures how well a company man-
ages its cash position, meaning how well the company generates cash to
pay its debt obligations and fund its operating expenses. The cash flow
statement complements the balance sheet and income statement and is
a mandatory part of a company's financial reports since 1987.[10]

The statement of cash flow is a popular report for investors and cred-
itors alike to help detect the health of the organization. The cash flow
statement can help detect unusual spending and also signal potential
future cash shortages.

Cash flow statements are made up of three parts:

1. Operating cash flow: This section summarizes the cash inflow and
   outflow related to the organization's primary operations. It would
   include money going out the door for COGS, personnel, and general
   and administrative spending. It summarizes activities related to current assets and liabilities.
2. Investing cash flow: This section summarizes cash impacting activities related to purchasing or disposing of investments, acquisitions,
   and so on.
3. Financing cash flow: This section summarizes gains from stock
   investments (dividends, etc.), additional investments, sale of stocks,
   and so on. It also covers issuance of debt and proceeds from those
   activities. This section also includes payments the organization may
   make as part of a dividend disbursement, if it pays dividends.

Cash is the lifeblood of any organization. Too little cash can slow or
stop operations altogether. The value of understanding where an organization's cash is coming from and going to cannot be understated. This
statement, along with the other two reports (balance sheet and income
statement), are vital windows into the health of any organization and
becoming familiar with these statements is valuable.

Financial Tools for PMs

In this section, we will review several calculations that are of value to project and program managers, as well as anyone interested in understanding how money and investing works. As with most concepts in this book, you may need to do additional study to really master them.

Present Value

Present value (PV) represents the value of a future stream of income in today's dollars. PV is used to decide if it is better to take a reduced payment now, or a set of payments in the future. Mortgage lenders, annuity companies, and other organizations use tools like PV to structure their product offerings to be profitable. This is also why the fine print in lotteries and sweepstakes offer the winners either an ongoing payment or a lump sum. The lump sum payment is always less than the sum of all the future payments, but in real terms (accounting for the time value of money), they should be the same. PV helps you understand this concept.

To understand PV better, let's imagine you owe a friend $1,000, and it's due in a year. You would rather just pay it off now, but feel you should pay a little less because you've learned about the time value of money. You want to propose a fair value to your friend if you pay today. You feel like 6 percent is a fair rate of return for your friend. How much should you propose to pay? To determine the answer, let's use the formula for PV:

$$PV = C/(1+i)^n$$

C = Amount of future payment

i = Interest rate

n = Number of payment periods

In our case, we know the C ($1,000), and you believe 6 percent is fair, so that is i. The number of periods will be one, as we are calculating the annual percentage rate. When we run the numbers, we get $943.39. So, if your friend is enlightened and understands the time value of money, he may take the offer if he believes that 6 percent is a fair return.

Be aware that there are dozens of online calculators that will help you determine PV. To use them, however, it's critical to understand the components that go into them; thus, I believe understanding the underlying formula is useful.

The importance of PV to project and program managers will become clear when we examine net present value (NPV), a common tool for judging the value a project will deliver.

Future Value

The future value (FV) formula is useful for determining the value of an investment at a future date given a specific interest rate. For this example, let's assume a friend wants to borrow $1,000, with a promise to pay you back in five years. You are happy to help the friend but expect a return on your loan of 6 percent per year. You want to know how much you will receive at the end of the loan. Your friend will not make any payments during the loan, it will be a lump sum at the end of the loan. The formula for FV is:

$$FV = PV(1+i)^t$$

PV = Present value (value today)

i = Interest rate for a specified period (we will use annual in this example)

t = Number of periods

Note that the preceding formula is for compound interest, meaning the interest is calculated annually, so each period the number increases (as opposed to simple interest where the interest is calculated once).

In our example where you loan your friend money, we know that PV = $1,000, i = 6 percent, and t = five years. Running the numbers, we get: $1,338.23.

As with PV (and most of the formulas presented in this book), there are many online resources to help you calculate FV. Understanding how the overall formula works is still valuable and will help us understand the next tool, NPV, which uses similar underlying formulas and inputs.

Net Present Value

Now that we know a little about PV and FV, we can better understand the power of NPV and its application to project and program management. NPV is important enough to project and program management that the Project Management Institute (PMI) has test questions on their Project

Management Professional (PMP) exam to ensure potential project managers understand the concept.

What is NPV, and what is it used for? NPV helps management understand the potential payout of a particular investment or project. There are

---

Overactive NPV:

The first time I used NPV in a professional setting was as part of a decision on whether to purchase a new software product. The chief information officer (CIO) wanted to better understand department costs and break them into operational buckets. We identified a market-leading tool that would automate this process and wanted to determine whether the value we expected was going to be worth the cost. It was an expensive tool, especially when I started to add in the costs associated new headcount required to manage and support the tool.

The benefits we expected were real but were hard to estimate. In my analysis, I estimated multiple cost efficiencies, savings the tool would likely identify, and several other factors.

In all, the spreadsheet was multiple tabs, and dozens of assumptions, and produced a solid NPV that supported purchase of the tool. The analysis took weeks to develop and was as meticulously detailed as I could make it. When I presented this data to the CIO, she was impressed but amused. She had never seen such a detailed attempt to develop an NPV, and while she could not argue with the results, it just didn't fit the budget and the tool was not funded. The entire effort was dismissed in less than 30 minutes of discussion.

I later learned from talking to others who develop NPV analyses that most executives are looking for solid but simple assumptions and a quick turnaround.

The lesson I wanted to share in this vignette is that NPV is a great tool, but don't let your insecurities about doing it *right* cause you to overshoot the mark. Solid and justifiable analysis is more important that tons of detail and cool spreadsheet tricks. Ultimately, leaders just want data to help them make their decisions.

other financial analyses that also help leaders with investment decisions such as ROI, internal rate of return (IRR) and payback method.

Let's look at the definition of NPV:

Net present value (NPV) is the difference between the present value of cash inflows and the present value of cash outflows over a period of time. NPV is used in capital budgeting and investment planning to analyze the profitability of a projected investment or project.[11]

As NPV results in an actual dollar figure, it is easy to compare the value of one project from another: The higher the NPV, the better the expected value. If an option returns a negative NPV, the investment would not return enough value to be worth the investment. With NPV, the minimum acceptable return is included in the calculation because you set an internal *hurdle* or target investment rate. For example, an organization may have a standard investment or hurdle rate of 9 percent. This means it only considers investing in projects that will return at least 9 percent. NPV will use that 9 percent as part of the calculation, and if the NPV is positive, then the investment will make more than 9 percent minimum return. If the NPV is negative, it means the hurdle rate was not met.

Take a simple example: Assume an organization is looking at two potential projects, Project A and Project B. Both projects will require a $100,000 initial investment and will return value to the company over three years. The company has an internal hurdle rate of 9 percent. Look at the data in Table 3.2.

Project A has a total return that is equal to the initial investment ($100,000). Due to the company's hurdle rate and the time value of money, the NPV is less than the initial investment; thus, management should not proceed with Project A.

Table 3.2 Project NPV Example 1

Option	Investment	Year 1 return	Year 2 return	Year 3 return	Total return	NPV
Project A	–$100,000	$20,000	$30,000	$50,000	$100,000	$82,208
Project B	–$100,000	$30,000	$40,000	$50,000	$120,000	$99,799

Table 3.3 Project NPV Example 2

Option	Investment	Year 1 return	Year 2 return	Year 3 return	Total return	NPV
Project C	–$200,000	$40,000	$80,000	$120,000	$240,000	$196,694
Project D	–$200,000	$120,000	$80,000	$40,000	$240,000	$208,313

Project B, on the other hand, has a total return of $120,000, but note that the NPV is still less than the initial investment. This project should not be invested in either. The project does not meet the minimum investment hurdle.

Let's look at two more projects, Project C and Project D. The company's hurdle remains the same at 9 percent, and the projects pay off over three years. Look at the data in Table 3.3.

Note that both projects have a total return over three years of $240,000. But Project C's NPV is less than its initial investment and should not be funded. Project D, with the same overall total return and the same hurdle rate, has an NPV greater than the initial investment and *should* be funded. Why the difference? Project D is more attractive because the returns are higher in the first and second year. Due to the time value of money, returns that come in early are worth more than those that come in later.

In most ways, NPV is like PV, except that NPV can account for varied future returns, whereas PV can only handle a constant future return. The formula for NPV is complex, and I would not recommend trying to calculate it by hand, especially when spreadsheets and online calculators do a great job of simplifying the work.

Return on Investment (ROI)

ROI is a phrase that is both a *concept* and a specific *formula* used to determine what investments should be made. As a concept, it's about getting more back than you invest. The term ROI is sometimes used to mean any calculation that helps determine what the FV of an investment is likely to be (or it can be used retrospectively to analyze past investment). But ROI is also a very specific calculation that returns a percentage. The power of

ROI is it is simple to understand. If you have an ROI of 5 percent, that is simple to understand.

Here is a definition for ROI:

Return on Investment (ROI) is a performance measure used to evaluate the efficiency of an investment or compare the efficiency of a number of different investments. ROI tries to directly measure the amount of return on a particular investment, relative to the investment's cost. To calculate ROI, the benefit (or return) of an investment is divided by the cost of the investment. The result is expressed as a percentage or a ratio.[12]

ROI contrasts to NPV, in that NPV uses a built-in target for a return, then tells us in dollars how much more than the hurdle rate the investment will return. ROI returns a percentage, and management will need to determine if that ROI is sufficient for investment.

Let's look at the formula for ROI:

$$ROI = (Current\ Value\ of\ Investment - Cost\ of\ Investment)/Cost\ of\ Investment$$

Here is a simple example: You work for a publicly traded company. You believe company leadership is making smart decisions and running the company well, so you invest $1,000 in company stock. One year later, you sell your stock for $1,100. Based on the preceding formula, your current investment is $1,100, and $1,000 was the cost of the investment. Your ROI is 10 percent. That is an obvious example that you probably did in your head. Look at another example in Table 3.4; this time two different projects your company is considering funding:

Table 3.4 Project ROI example

Project name	Investment required	Expected return	Investment length	ROI
Project 1	$200,000	$250,000	1 year	25%
Project 2	$500,000	$750,000	3 years	50%

ROI tells us we should invest in Project 2, but have you detected any issues with that option? The first issue is that Project 2 takes more than twice the investment of Project 1. The second issue is that the calculation does not account for the fact the return does not come until Year 3 (time value of money again!). To make up for that shortcoming, you could look at an average yearly yield of Project 2. If you did, you'd discover the annual yield is just 16.67 percent, making Project 1 a much better investment option. ROI is great because of its simplicity, but if you choose to use it, be aware of its shortcomings.

Internal Rate of Return (IRR)

IRR is closely related to NPV. What IRR does differently than NPV is it returns a percentage instead of a dollar amount. It does this by setting the NPV to zero, allowing the percentage to be derived.

The definition of IRR is:

The internal rate of return is a metric used in financial analysis to estimate the profitability of potential investments. The internal rate of return is a discount rate that makes the net present value (NPV) of all cash flows equal to zero in a discounted cash flow analysis. IRR calculations rely on the same formula as NPV does.[13]

Let's use the same preceding project examples from NPV. As with NPV, the formula for IRR is complicated, and the most direct, practical way to derive IRR is in a spreadsheet or an online calculator. See Table 3.5.

As expected, IRR shows that Project B is the better option of these two projects. Table 3.6 shows IRR for preceding Projects C and D.

Table 3.5 Project IRR Example 1

Option	Investment	Year 1 return	Year 2 return	Year 3 return	Total return	IRR
Project A	–$100,000	$20,000	$30,000	$50,000	$100,000	0%
Project B	–$100,000	$30,000	$40,000	$50,000	$120,000	8.9%

Table 3.6 Project IRR Example 2

Option	Investment	Year 1 return	Year 2 return	Year 3 return	Total return	IRR
Project C	–$200,000	$40,000	$80,000	$120,000	$240,000	8.2%
Project D	–$200,000	$120,000	$80,000	$40,000	$240,000	11.8%

As the IRR formula is sensitive enough to detect accelerated payback, Project D becomes the clear winner of the four projects. Note that Project D is the only project to show an IRR above the internal hurdle rate of 9 percent—which is why the NPV calculation showed it as the only positive value.

Bonus Section: Behavioral Finance

One of my very favorite classes at Haas was a *behavioral* finance class. Not only was the professor exceptional, the subject matter was a refreshing contrast to the more buttoned-down finance and accounting curriculum. I want to share a few of the teachings from this class that have stayed with me throughout the years. The application of these teachings to project and program management is more about managing human nature than financial figures. Consider this an *elective* course within the chapter and an advertisement for the more fun aspects of MBA programs.

Behavioral finance is the study of individual behavior of investors and financial analysts. It turns on its head one of the common mantras about the market—that it is strictly rational. Behavioral finance is a psychological and sociological look at the workings of investor and analyst minds as they examine financial opportunities.

The following are some common principles of behavioral finance.

Anchoring

Anchoring is a psychological concept that says an individual tends to focus on one (usually the first) piece of information they hear about a particular subject. In finance, this means that if someone says a stock is a good deal at $50 per share, then you will view that stock's price through that lens even when that anchor number is no longer realistic.

This is an extremely valuable concept to understand as a project and program manager because the first date or budget estimate that comes out of your mouth will have an outsized influence on the perceived success of your project. For example, if you tell your stakeholders you think you can finish the project in two months, even if you give a lot of *caveats* to that estimate, the stakeholders will most likely use that two-month estimate as the yardstick for success. The same goes for budget estimates. In practice, I try to avoid giving any estimates whatsoever for as long as possible to avoid stakeholder disappointment, as date and budget estimates change over time. When I do give estimates, I share only the top range first because it is always an easier conversation to say something will be done sooner and for less money than the other way around.

Herd Mentality

This is an interesting principle that shows up in a lot of areas in life. It is the result of social pressure people feel to do what those around them are doing. In the financial world, this behavior often manifests in market bubbles. From the centuries-old tulip bulb bubble in Holland, to real estate and stock market bubbles, there is an instinct that drives people to want to jump on the same investing strategy as others. These bubbles start with sound thinking and are, at the start, a good place to put an investment. But herd mentality can cause others to seek those initial returns long after the intrinsic value of the investment has been eclipsed by the market price. As market price drives higher, more people invest in the asset, further increasing the gap between the real value and the market value of the underlying asset.

I see some of this herd mentality in the pursuit of some project management certifications. The first to get certified in agile methodologies likely saw great ROI. As more and more people piled in to get their certifications, the overall value of the certifications has been diluted. Do I believe there is a bubble in certifications? Not really, but I do see herd mentality in some aspects of the certification mills that have been established in our profession.

Loss Aversion

Loss aversion is one of the funnier idiosyncrasies found in humans. The principle says that people feel more pain with a loss, than with the equivalent amount of gain. In fact, Nobel prize winner Daniel Kahneman and his partner Amos Tversky estimated that the amount of pain of a loss is about two times greater than the pleasure of a gain.[14] Let's use this example to illustrate: Your friend tells you he will give you $100 if you flip a coin and get heads. You will lose $100 if you get tails. Would you do it? The loss aversion theory says you likely won't do it. The chances of winning would have to outweigh the loss by a factor of two before most people would start to take the deal.

All this is to say people have a strong aversion to loss. This helps us to explain why conversations with our project stakeholders are always difficult when we are reducing scope in a project. There is an innate aversion to receiving less than the anchored (see above!) expectation. Even if we promise to give them more of a different type of scope, the weight of the loss will be significant. When working with stakeholders, managers, and others, always keep in mind how powerful the effect of loss aversion can be as you make decisions to communicate.

Familiarity Bias

Familiarity bias is the tendency to stay within familiar patterns and within what is known and recognized.[15] For example, when facing something new or unseen, the mind will automatically look for patterns from past experience to help explain the situation and give the person a familiar frame of reference. This is very efficient and psychologically comforting but can lead to a person staying within a narrow frame of reference. As it relates to finance, this means that people typically only invest in a few, familiar areas of the market.

Familiarity bias impacts project and program managers in the same way it affects everyone else. If we were successfully using a certain strategy in the past, we will likely try to apply the same strategy to future challenges, even if the situation calls for new or different thinking. To protect against this bias in our profession, it is good to engage in continuous learning.

Attending lectures or conferences, reading books and articles, gaining additional education (such as an MBA), and anything that opens the mind to new ideas will help keep your mind more pliable. The more open and pliable a person is, the less likely familiarity bias will impact them.

Mental Accounting

It turns out that the way people account for money inside their mind is strangely inconsistent. Think about your income from work. Some professionals receive bonuses and stock options in addition to their regular income. Typically, people will allocate their regular income to paying rent, groceries, insurance, gas, and the basic costs of living. People are very protective of their income and will conserve and reduce the expenses paid from their incomes. On the other hand, bonus and stock grants are more typically used for vacations, investments, and other less typical expenses. Why is that? A dollar from income or bonus has the same value, but in our minds, we have compartmentalized the way we think about financial matters. Similarly, people will be more inclined to drive across town to save $5.00 on a $15.00 item, but less inclined to take the same drive save $5.00 on a $125.00 item. It's the same $5.00 savings either way. Some financial resources are viewed as more valuable than others. It is completely irrational, but it's part of our make-up.

What does this mean for project and program management professionals? I have seen a lot of evidence of mental accounting as it relates to internal and external personnel resources. Managers tend to give a lot of scrutiny to the use of outside resources while treating costs for internal employees with less attention. This is because employees are seen as part of the company structure, whereas outside contractors are seen as cash outflows. The costs are often the same.

As stewards of an organization's resources, we must do what we can to eliminate mental accounting biases and represent the true costs of projects.

Gambler's Fallacy

Imagine you have a quarter in your hand. You flip it and get heads. You flip it another nine times, you get heads each time. You are probably thinking that when you flip it again, you are bound to get tails, after all, you're *due*. The problem is, the odds of you getting heads on the next flip is the same as it's been the 10 previous times: 50 percent. Gamblers often think in terms of recent streaks to incorrectly predict odds of things. It is a fallacy to think you are due for a different outcome if the odds of that outcome are no different than previous plays.

Whether you're a gambler looking to break a losing streak or working with other statistically consistent processes, keep this mental bias in your head as a warning that our minds tend to disregard facts for odd mental biases such as the gambler's fallacy.

Application to Project and Program Managers

The study of finance is rich with principles and tools for project and program managers. There is a reason I put the study of finance near the beginning of the book because I believe familiarity with it is essential to project and program managers who want to advance in their careers. Whether it is understanding the basic vocabulary and concepts of finance so you can be more effective in your role, or diving deeper into the world of finance because you are managing a program within that area, studying the basics of finance is rewarding personally and professionally.

Understanding the basic financial reports of a company will help you understand how your project rolls up to the larger financial picture. It can also help you be a smarter personal investor, should you choose to invest. Being able to calculate PV, FV, NPV, ROI, and IRR can help set you apart as a project and program manager. These skills may not be used every day, but when they are needed, it is important to have a working knowledge of what is needed.

Additional Resources

Free corporate finance textbook (requires sending your e-mail address): https://book.ivo-welch.info/home/

Free online financial accounting textbook: https://open.lib.umn.edu/financialaccounting/

CHAPTER 4

Corporate Accounting

Why Study Accounting?

I took my first accounting class as part of my undergraduate minor program. I was not going to become an accountant, but I had always been curious what the field entailed and was excited to learn more. At the time I did not know what a *weed-out* class was, but after just a few weeks of this accounting course I became very familiar with the term. A weed-out class is one that is purposely difficult within a major to help weed out prospective students who are just not suited to the field. After scratching out what seemed like my thousandth T-account in that class, all curiosity was quenched. I wanted nothing to do with accounting. When the time came for my MBA-level accounting class, I was nervous because of past experience, but that nervousness was unfounded because it turns out when a professor is more interested in teaching and less concerned about discouraging students—the field is actually not so bad.

For those not familiar with the field of accounting, it may seem like accounting and finance are the same thing. Both are fundamental organizational functions that focus on numbers and reporting and both follow extensive rules from governing bodies. But they are really quite different disciplines. As stated in the previous chapter, I think of finance as a discipline that recommends and plans where an organization's money should go, and accounting is the discipline that counts and reports where the money went. While there is more to it than this, the sentiment captures the fact that accounting is a recording function for the money.

Accounting intersects with project and program management in some significant ways. First, it is likely that as you take on projects with budget components, you may be asked to supply data to accounting. One of the common requests made by accountants to project managers is for expense accruals. If you have not run into accruals, you might, so learning about them is a good idea. Additionally, your project may be classified as a *capital* project, which requires more careful tracking and reporting of budget spend. Also, there may be a point in your career where you become an independent project consultant and then understanding accounts payable (AP) and accounts receivable (AR) processes can be incredibly useful. There are other possible intersects as well, as you will see in this chapter.

Understanding the Basics

Stereotypes of accounting (and accountants) abound. From the outside, it looks a lot like crunching numbers all day, and it is, but there are a lot of nuances to the profession. One of the first things to realize is that there is more than one type of accounting. We will look at the two primary types in Table 4.1.

Financial accounting is important because it ties to the financial success of the business, whereas managerial accounting is important because it enables management make important decisions (which should then impact the financial success of the business!). Together they form an important set of management tools with which all project and program managers should be familiar.

Let's examine both types of accounting referenced a little more carefully.

Table 4.1 Types of accounting

Type of accounting	Definition
Financial accounting	Financial accounting is a specific branch of accounting involving a process of recording, summarizing, and reporting the myriad of transactions resulting from business operations over a period of time. These transactions are summarized in the preparation of financial statements, including the balance sheet, income statement, and cash flow statement, that record the company's operating performance over a specified period.[1]
Managerial accounting	Managerial accounting is the practice of identifying, measuring, analyzing, interpreting, and communicating financial information to managers for the pursuit of an organization's goals. It varies from financial accounting because the intended purpose of managerial accounting is to assist users internal to the company in making well-informed business decisions.[2]

Financial Accounting

The principles of financial accounting are closely tied to those of corporate finance, and that makes sense because accounting tracks where money has been spent, and corporate finance directs where the money should be going. Financial accounting is bound by detailed rules and extensive regulatory oversight due to the public nature of the produced data. There are well-trod paths to producing financial reports, and those paths are lined with strong fencing. Even organizations that are not public will want to produce accurate financial reports based on a subset of the public rules.

The Role in Corporate America

Financial accounting gives investors, shareholders, government regulators, and others a window into the financial health of the company. Without a careful accounting and reporting of spend, there would be no way to compare quarter-over-quarter or year-over-year financial changes within an organization, nor an ability to compare one company's financial health to another's. The finance markets, as we know them, would be more akin to a game of blind darts than they already seem.

To get to the rolled-up numbers we see in company financial reports, accountants must use carefully established processes to track money moving into, and out of, the company. We will look at a few of these established processes next.

Accounts Receivable (AR)

AR refers to money that is owed to the organization but is not yet paid by the outside party. AR processes are very carefully managed and even show up on an organization's balance sheet as an asset. In larger organizations, there are teams of accountants focused on nothing but the tracking and reporting of money owed. In fact, something as seemingly simple as being able to say when an organization can report money from a sale (called revenue recognition) can be extraordinarily complex.

AR also has to deal with issues such as how long to allow a customer to pay a bill, what to do if a bill goes unpaid past a certain date, and when to write-off bad debt.

All receivables are tracked in an organization's general ledger (GL) as a *credit* on the right side.

Accounts Payable

AP is about paying an organization' liabilities or debts. If an organization makes cupcakes, it will have bills to pay such as facilities costs, raw ingredients, utilities, delivery costs, and so on. AP is all about preserving an organization's cash as long as possible. Some companies make a policy to pay their bills at (or sometimes beyond) the latest date required by a supplier. This keeps cash in the bank accounts as long as possible.

AP processes include setting up vendors in a system so that they can be paid, collecting invoices, sending payments, and the recording and coding of all expenses paid. All expenses paid are bucketed into a select few accounts so that organizations can report how much they paid for specific spend categories such as transportation, travel, cost of goods sold, salary, benefits, and so on.

The entire foundation of financial reporting starts with the coding of individual costs in the company's GL. AP transactions are recorded as *debits* on the left side of the GL.

As a project or program manager, you may be called on to manage budgets that contain external expenses such as vendor contracts, travel, hardware, or consulting resources. All of these costs will be processed through AP, and you as the project manager may be called on to help approve, manage, or explain details related to the costs so that the AP accountants can categorize it properly. Of note, all employee salaries are an expense as well. Unless you are managing a capital project or the organization uses time cards to track where time goes, you may not have much to do with the tracking and reporting of this expense.

General Ledger

An organization's GL is an ongoing record of all financial transactions at a detailed level. Every box of pencils purchased, every major sale of a product—it's all recorded on the GL. Each entry of the GL contains a credit and debit entry to place the entry into the right accounting bucket. If you are familiar with the idea of system or database logs, it's a similar concept. All financial transactions are recorded in the GL. If the transactions are recorded properly, a company can see their financial picture in great detail.

In modern companies, a GL can grow daily by thousands of lines, and in larger companies, many accountants won't deal directly with the GL; there is a dedicated team for the ledger. As a project manager, you probably won't have much interaction with the ledger either unless you are working as a PM within a finance team that is working on the GL.

Capital Versus Expense

As has been stated in other sections of this book, project costs are broken into capital expenditure (sometimes called CapEx) or operational expense (sometimes called OpEx). As a reminder from Chapter 3 *Corporate Finance*, the difference between these is that expenses immediately leave the organization's balance sheet, whereas capital expenditures remain an asset of the company on the balance sheet until they are fully depreciated over their useful lives. As capital sits on the balance sheet, a company can look like it has a healthier ratio of assets to liabilities when a lot of purchases are capitalized. Some companies use this to their advantage. Others have learned that when you capitalize too many costs, the associated depreciation can have negative impacts on earnings. It boils down to whether an organization prefers to take the full impact of an expense up front, or over time.

I was first introduced to capital projects when I was an independent consultant to a publicly traded company. This company favored capital projects whenever they could justify them. It was a great engagement that I wanted to keep going as long as possible so I found that if I could help management package their project ideas in such a way that accounting would be able to classify them as capital, I could move from one project to another. It worked out well for the company and for me.

The following is an illustration of why managers often prefer to capitalize projects, but it also shows why capitalizing can be a budget trap:

A department has a $10M annual budget. After headcount and other expenses, it has $1M available to fund an important project. If the project will be expensed, the department can spend $1M this year on the project. Simple. If the project can be capitalized and depreciated over three years, the department can spend $3M on the project because a maximum of $1M will hit the budget this year as depreciation. Why would a manager do anything but capitalize projects? Because the following year budget still has to carry the burden of the depreciation from the prior year. If the department gets the same budget the following year and carves out the same project budget of $1M, that $1M is already spent on depreciation, and they cannot do any additional project work that year (and possibly the next).

When determining whether a project can be fully or partially capitalized, you may be asked to break down several components:

- The amount and kind of labor needed. Whether the labor is employees or not, and whether the overall cost of labor meets a certain threshold
- The amount and kind of software involved
- The amount and kind of hardware involved
- Improvements to physical facilities

One of the nuances to capital projects is that they may be capitalized in increments during project execution, or all at once when execution is completed. Pushing the asset into service (capitalizing it) means that the value of the asset moves places on the balance sheet. If all or part of your project can be capitalized, be prepared to answer questions from accounting so that they can help determine when and how much moves into service.

Rules around capitalization can be tricky. For example, a company may have a $5,000 threshold before data center equipment can be capitalized. This is to keep small items such as hard drives from being capitalized (and cause an accountant to have to track that asset). But the same company may say that an aggregate order of equipment that exceeds $5,000 can be capitalized. So, if a company orders 10 $500 disks, the 10 disks could be capitalized depending on the rule.

Capitalizing Memory

Early in my career, I worked for a company that was struggling financially and started to capitalize equipment as much as possible. This led to ridiculous conversations with our accounting team. Capital equipment is often tracked with physical labels as part of the asset tracking rules established by accounting. However, when we would order new memory chips that could be capitalized, we would also be given large, sticky labels to put on the memory chips to track them. Not only would these labels not even fit on the chips, but even if they had, they would be hidden deep within the chassis of the computer server, and they would affect the thermal properties of the chip as the label glue would melt with the high temperatures. We had lengthy conversations about options, and while we eventually ended up getting accounting to reverse their label policies for small items, for a time, we had to stick labels on some really unusual items.

Expense-only projects are much simpler from an accounting standpoint. Newer cloud companies sometimes prefer the cleanliness of expensing all but the largest purchases. It also avoids the budget trap that depreciation can create with capital projects. If your project(s) are expense-only, your burden to report to accounting is much reduced.

Depreciation

The reason an organization capitalizes an asset is because the asset still provides value to the organization, so eliminating the value of the asset by expensing it may not fairly represent reality. Think about an organization that purchases a delivery truck. This truck is key to delivering products to customers, and at any given time, the truck has value until it reaches its end-of-life. Depreciation is the mechanism accountants use to decrease—or depreciate—the value of the asset to more closely resemble its real-world value. Accountants will establish depreciation schedules depending on the type of asset. Laptops may be three years, servers five years, vehicles seven years, and so on.

If you reach the point in your career when you are managing portfolios and their associated budget, you may need to understand the impact of depreciation more carefully than at other times in your career. The treatment of depreciation can swing an organization's budget by a significant amount. When managing department budgets, I have been both saved by depreciation windfalls and hurt by budget shortfalls caused by depreciation changes.

Accruals

Accountants have a principle called the *matching principle*, which states that when expenses are incurred, they need to be reflected in the same accounting period. While the principle makes a lot of sense, it is actually trickier to implement than it may seem. For example, if you use outside consultants for any work, they will likely send you a monthly invoice for work done the prior month. The matching principle says that the cost of that consulting should be reflected in the same month it was incurred. How can you reflect un-invoiced work in the month it was incurred? Accruals. Accruals are an accounting device that plugs the books with estimates for costs until the actual costs are able to be recorded.

I've had to submit accrual estimates for years at some companies, as a project manager. The procedure is not complicated but has to be done with some precision. At or near the end of the month, you may need to reach out to each vendor working on your project to ask for their estimates on what they will be charging for that month. Sometimes consultants don't actually know the rate at which they are being billed, so it may be up to you to find the hours they worked, then multiply the hours by their rate to derive your accrual amount.

Some accountants are good about reminding project managers when accruals are due, others will tell you once about the expectation, then expect you to send them in on a regular schedule. As gathering the data can sometimes take a day or two, I will set up a calendar reminder to keep me on track. Missing an accrual is a big deal in the accounting world, so you want to prioritize accruals if they are required for your project.

Managerial Accounting

Managerial accounting, sometimes called cost accounting, is the branch of accounting that enables managers to make really effective business decisions around key operations. Unlike financial accounting, managerial accounting is about analyzing cost data for the benefit of business decisions. In my opinion, as a manager within a corporate organization, I find managerial accounting more interesting and applicable to running and managing a business.

Managerial accounting breaks cost data into fixed and variable costs, direct and indirect costs (sometimes called overhead), and manufacturing and non-manufacturing costs. This allows management to build analyses that reflect full costs of various products and projects.

There are a few traditional decision points that managerial accounting helps facilitate:

Marginal Analysis

This is the study of the impact of increased production. What does it cost to manufacture one more unit, or 1,000 more units? Marginal analysis can answer that question. It also answers the question at what point a company breaks even in its manufacturing. This is a critical piece of data for a company to calculate as it contemplates whether a new product line is likely to pay off, and by how much.

Cost Accounting

Sometimes called activity-based accounting (ABC), it is the study of component costs for products and projects within an organization. The complexity of cost accounting comes with treatment of *overhead* costs such as human resources (HR), information technology (IT), and finance support costs. These services are not directly used in the creation of a product but are required for the running of the business. Cost accounting derives ways to allocate these costs so that a complete cost picture can be painted. Cost accounting empowers management to see data more clearly and make important decisions.

Transfer Pricing

When one department of an organization relies on the products or services of another department, the organization needs to determine a fair cost to charge for that transfer. It might sound easy, but there is a lot of subtlety in these calculations. Take an automobile manufacturer. They may have a department dedicated to producing engines. If the cost for this depart- ment to produce an engine is $500, what is the internal transfer cost of that engine to the assembly department? Major considerations in answering this question include where the manufacturing takes place and the associated tax implications. For example, if the engine department is in Japan, but the final automobile manufacturing takes place in the United States, there are implications for importing the engines into the country. Transfer pricing takes into account all of the key factors and produces a transfer price that is best for the organization.

Cost of Inventory

If we continue the automobile manufacturing example introduced in the preceding section, we can illustrate the importance of getting the cost of inventory correct. At any given time, the manufacturer will have a supply of engines, a supply of bodies, car frames, electronic harnesses, seats, and so on. These will be assembled together at some point, but until then, these components may sit waiting for completion. These components have some value, so the question becomes: What is the value of a partially assembled automobile? Finding the right answer to that question is important because that automobile manufacturer will have a sizeable line on the balance sheet titled Work in Progress (WIP) or something similar. Managerial accounting uses various tools to help an organization determine and manage inventory costs.

Application to Project and Program Management

Projects, and thus project managers, consume resources to create a result that is greater than the component parts. Identifying, tracking, and reporting on project costs is vital to understanding and controlling the organization budget. The larger the budget a project or program manager is responsible for, the greater the need to understand accounting principles and communicate effectively with your accounting partner. It is vital that project and program managers stay aligned with their accounting partners on cost tracking and reporting when managing projects.

As shown in this chapter, the application of accounting to project and program management intersects at several places, including the inclusion of project costs in financial and managerial accounting reports. Ensuring accurate costing is not just important, it is an obligation of project and program managers as stewards of an organization's resources. In order to effectively communicate project expenses, a project and program manager needs to have at least a working knowledge of basic accounting processes covered in this chapter.

Of course, the more accounting knowledge a project and program professional has, the more valuable they become to the organization. The project and program manager with this knowledge will become trusted to run increasingly costly projects because of the professional way budget matters were managed and communicated.

Additional Resources

A free, interactive website that contains an entire accounting textbook, complete with problems and solutions: https://principlesofaccounting. com

A free textbook that is part of a large library of university-level textbooks: https://open.umn.edu/opentextbooks/textbooks/accounting-principles-a-business-perspective

A free online textbook for managerial accounting: https://scholarsarchive.library.albany.edu/cgi/viewcontent. cgi?article=1000&context=accounting_fac_books

CHAPTER 5

Operations Management

Why Study Operations Management?

In some ways, operations management is the opposite of project management. The objective of operations management is to refine and perfect repeatable processes. It is about keeping processes and systems stable, consistent, and always available. The objective of project and program management is to develop and introduce new or changed processes and technologies. It is about disrupting and changing the status quo. Projects are temporary endeavors. Operations management focuses on ongoing processes. This is why a project implementation plan is so critical, it helps transition the new process or technology into the existing operational landscape with the goal of adding new capabilities, tools, processes, and technologies.

So, why study operations management as a project manager? For three primary reasons:

1. Understanding the environment into which you will deploy your project is essential to program success. This chapter will describe common operations management concepts that may increase your knowledge and success in future projects.

2. One of the ways I have seen program managers deployed is to manage regular, repeatable bodies of work. This is more akin to operations management than project management. Examples include annual audit oversight, regular planning processes, review cycles, and so on. Some program managers work exclusively on work that directly intersects with operational duties, such as new product introduction (NPI) or mergers and acquisitions (M&A), and, thus, can learn from operations management.

3. Some operations management experts (and text books) include project management as a core competency within the operations

management field. While I agree that project management competency is important in operations, I am not sure I agree it lives within the subset of operations management.

Operations management is a core MBA topic and something about which all business-savvy employees should develop a working knowledge.

Understanding the Basics

The history of operations management starts in the earliest days of the industrial revolution. Production techniques were largely manual and not terribly efficient at the start. Typically, the items being produced would be stationary, and the production workers would move around to do their work. This changed when assembly lines were invented. While Henry Ford did not invent assembly lines, his use of them was an early success story. He set up his automobile factory in a moving assembly line where he had workers stay in their areas and the automobile components would travel to them. This radically changed production capacity for automobiles. The foundations of manufacturing operations changed forever with the adoption of these practices.

Today, manufacturing organizations study and measure every motion required to make a product and continuously work to streamline the manufacturing process. Reducing the number of steps, or reducing the time for a step in the process can yield enormous efficiencies, especially when the volume of products produced is large.

Modern operations management looks beyond just manufacturing. Companies that have no manufacturing capabilities often have operations teams that help manage business processes and services. Operations management is involved in process and service design, risk management, quality measurement and improvement, enterprise planning, supply chain, and other areas key to running a business. One of the primary missions of operations management is to make the organization more efficient. Each dollar saved directly impacts the organization's bottom-line financials.

A more recent evolution of operations management has to do with digital operations, or managing the organization in a paperless, data-driven way. The great thing about operations management is that the overall mission to drive efficiencies remains the same, but over decades, the tools and techniques used have evolved to keep up with business innovations. The remainder of this chapter will review the core principles of modern operations management.

Process Analysis and Design

Whether people think about it or not, an organization is made up of thousands of processes. Processes that seem basic or simple can actually have hundreds or thousands of subprocesses that support the primary processes. It is the job of operations experts to streamline, automate, and simplify these processes as much as possible.

Think about what it takes to cut a simple paycheck. First, a bank account needs to be set up and maintained, including managing who can access the account. Most larger organizations use direct deposit, so those processes must be established and communicated. Someone must calculate not just the paycheck amount, but how much federal, state, and local tax must be pulled. Those taxes must be collected, reported, and sent to the appropriate collection organizations. If the employer offers benefits such as health insurance, dental insurance, life insurance, retirement accounts, and similar, it must calculate, collect, and disposition each of those accounts. Once the amount of the paycheck is calculated, the check must be cut using whatever governance processes are required by the organization to ensure there is no abuse when issuing checks. All of the subprocesses required to cut a single check could number in the hundreds at larger organizations. It is no wonder that companies spend a significant time and money to continuously improve processes. In the case of paychecks, it has become common practice to outsource parts of the payroll process because they are not core to what most companies do. It makes more sense to pay someone else with expertise in that area to manage the processes for them.

Understanding what processes are core to an organization is one of the first discussions all organizations should have. If the company makes automobiles, then they will want to analyze and invest in making the manufacturing processes as efficient as possible. It is much less important for the automobile manufacturer to spend time and attention on processes such as payroll because these can be handed off to experts in that area. This allows the company to remain focused on its areas of competitive advantage.

Efficiency experts are sometimes hired to improve process efficiency. These experts will decompose all of the subprocesses, observe how they are run, measure current efficiency, and then make suggestions for improvement. Corporations such as General Electric developed entire training programs around process efficiency (called Six Sigma), with graduates certified at different *belt* levels that mirror martial arts achievements. The foundation of these programs is using lean process thinking and statistics to manage and improve processes.

Sometimes an organization does not have existing processes or is introducing a major change to existing process. This allows the company to design the process in question from the ground up. New processes are often designed and explained using workflow diagrams. Most project managers will be familiar with process workflow diagrams with their step-by-step mapping of process components.

Sometimes in large process changes (such as replacing an entire enterprise resource planning (ERP) system), the processes of an entire department are carefully blueprinted, then redesigned so that the new system will account for all of the many component processes.

Smaller organizations can get away with simpler processes at first. But as small organizations grow, they will have to add new processes and scale existing ones. A process that works for an organization with 50 people will not likely work for an organization with thousands of people. Process analysis and design are always taking place in organizations, and project and program managers are likely to be tasked with running processes re-design projects.

Risk Management

Another key responsibility of operations management is identifying, documenting, managing, and reporting on important risks that might impact an organization. Just as good project and program managers manage risk at a program level, operational risk management takes place at the organization level. Managing risk at the organizational level is often called enterprise risk management (ERM). The principles taught to project managers are largely the same as those used by enterprise risk managers. The definition of ERM is as follows:

Enterprise risk management (ERM) is a plan-based business strategy that aims to identify, assess, and prepare for any dangers, hazards, and other potentials for disaster—both physical and figurative—that may interfere with an organization's operations and objectives.[1]

Benefits of Risk Management

Risk management takes concerted effort on the part of the organization to do well, so why would it want to make the effort?

- ERM examines positive (upside) risk as well as negative risk, allowing for organizations to exploit identified opportunities to their benefit.
- Business operations become more stable and reliable over time.
- When risk is better quantified, it enables management to make better decisions.
- Improved compliance processes can reduce the overall costs of compliance.
- When risks do hit, the impact can reduce financial and reputational damage.

Fundamentals of Risk Management

Similar to project risk management, there are a few primary steps risk managers take to reduce risk.

Identifying Risk: Before a risk can be managed, it has to be identified and cataloged. Risks can come from anywhere, and experienced risk managers will look at many types of risks. Risks can be physical, financial, competitive, political, regulatory, security, and so on. Each type of risk will be written in a risk register to be assessed.

Assessing Risk: Once risks are identified, they are assessed for how likely they are to actually happen, as well as how impactful they will be if they do manifest. Risks that are likely to arise are prioritized for further analysis, as are those risks that, if they hit, would devastate the organization.

Planning for Mitigation: Organizations cannot plan for every kind of risk. It doesn't make financial sense to spend time on low-likelihood risk, or low-impact risks, but for those deemed worth further analysis, the organization can start to make plans for how it will respond. One of the more common methods to start risk planning is to decide whether the organization should take one of the following four actions:

1. *Accept Risk:* This is the simplest of actions and is a formal acknowledgment that the risk might happen, and if it does, the organization accepts the consequences. No additional action will be taken for this risk.

2. *Mitigate:* Mitigating the risk means the organization will take steps to reduce either the likelihood of the risk manifesting or reduce the impact if it happens. Mitigations could include adding safety processes or structures, increasing financial reserves, increasing patent protections, increasing security tools and monitoring, or many other mitigations.

3. *Transfer:* Some risks can be given to other organizations. This is most often accomplished through insurance. For example, if the risk of flooding is deemed large enough, an organization can choose to take out insurance against that risk. Other types of risk transfer can include using outsourcing organizations to do risky work.

4. *Avoid:* As it sounds, this means an organization will choose to step around the risk by stopping the activities that create the risk exposure. If the risk of government regulation is too large in a particular country, the organization may choose not to do business in that country, eliminating the risk.

For risks that are large enough, the organization may choose to do more detailed analysis and planning. Some organizations create full playbooks that they will activate should the risk manifest. One way of planning for major risks is to do business continuity planning (BCP). BCP sets up plans for how an organization will act when a major risk event takes place. This often includes impacts to headquarters, when executives have to be physically separated while maintaining control of the organization. BCP can include the loss of major business functions such as key information technology systems, major impacts to the workforce and their ability to do their work, loss of facilities, and other potentially catastrophic losses.

Monitoring and Reporting: Identifying and planning for risks does little good to the organization if the risk environment changes in the future, or the plans become outdated. Continuously monitoring for risk and remaining on the right footing to respond quickly to risk is part of a robust ERM program. Larger organizations may set up security operations centers where live camera feeds allow for centralized monitoring of physical assets such as buildings. Some functions within the organization, such as in finance, will monitor for financial risks, and security teams will monitor for security and data risks. Enterprise risk teams can bring all of these groups together when an event happens and coordinate a comprehensive response to lessen the impact.

Control

When a process is *in control* in an operations context, it is operating within pre-defined parameters. The National Institute of Standards and Technology defines control this way:

> *Process Control is the active changing of the process based on the results of process monitoring. Once the process monitoring tools have detected an out-of-control situation, the person responsible for the process makes a change to bring the process back into control.*[2]

Thus, when a process is in control, it is operating within expected standards and producing expected outcomes. When a process goes *out of control*, it no longer produces the expected outcome.

How does this apply to project and program management? As project and program managers, we work within a framework of processes. The goal of these processes is to improve outcomes and consistency. Think about what *control* means within the common processes used in your organization. What is the implication if you do not follow your organization's project reporting process? Would the needed status be available to leadership? Wouldn't this create an *out of control* situation where the process did not produce the intended outcome? As you think through existing processes, it may be helpful to think about the intended outcomes and what happens when they are (or are not) producing expected outcomes.

This exercise becomes more powerful when you are creating or modifying processes to improve them. As you develop new processes, think about what the ideal, or in-control, state is. Then, think about what out of control would look like, and what you would need to do to bring the process back into control. The processes you create will become more meaningful as you consider the concept of control.

Quality Management

Occasionally, when I buy a new item of clothing, I will find a small piece of paper tucked in the clothing that says "Inspected by," and then a person's name or identification number. This is meant to show a consumer that the company has a strong quality program because the item was inspected. However, quality practitioners will recognize the flaw in this. Quality should be built into the system from the start of the process so that post-manufacturing inspection is not required (or minimally required). This is where a good project manager can be invaluable—by including quality as one of the key pillars of project delivery.

One of the principal founders of the modern quality movement is W. Edwards Deming. Deming, an engineer and statistician, found enormous success in Japan and helped transition their struggling automobile manufacturing sector into an international juggernaut known for the quality of its automobiles. Deming introduced many of the key quality principles that are still in use today, including the Deming wheel.

Deming Wheel

The key steps to ensuring quality outcomes include Plan, Do, Study, Act, which form a virtuous cycle. Each step is briefly outlined as follows:

1. *Plan:* This step includes identifying the area to improve, collecting data, and developing a plan for the improvement.

2. *Do:* This step involved implementing the plan, then collecting data on whether the plan has actually improved the quality of the output.
3. *Study:* This step is about analyzing the new data and comparing it to the original data.
4. *Act:* If data shows the plan has improved quality, continue with the plan. If not, make adjustments, collect new data, and do additional analysis.

By using the principles of the Deming wheel when implementing change, you can bolster odds of success with that change.

There are many key contributors to modern quality practices besides Deming. It is worth briefly mentioning at least two more because the organization you work for may have been influenced by their contributions. One is the work of Joseph Juran, who was a major force in spreading the Pareto principle across the United States and the industrial world. The other is Kaizen, a Japanese principle of continuous improvement. Japanese auto manufacturer Toyota adopted the principles of Kaizen as part of their quality drive decades ago. The principle of Kaizen includes making small but meaningful changes that can create great impact over time.

Supply Chain Management

Supply chain management (SCM) focuses on ensuring the materials and raw ingredients needed to create the organizations' products are available in the quantities needed, at the quality needed, and at the time needed for business operations. It also includes storage of products as they are in mid-assembly, which is called work in progress (WIP). Supply chain includes the logistics of shipping and receiving goods, ensuring items received are up to the specification required, return of defective items, and storage of supplies waiting for assembly.

Project and program management is dependent on, and a beneficiary of, SCM. Many of the inputs we need to deliver our projects may be a product of SCM. It is interesting to note that projects also have the concept of *work in progress* to express the state between raw ingredient and finished product. Project and SCM disciplines have many common connections and dependencies on each other.

In stable economic times, with solid transportation distribution channels, SCM focuses on optimizing supply chains. Other times, such as during the Covid-19 pandemic, supply chains were disrupted, creating shortages in many products. From toilet paper, to disinfecting supplies, to flour—the demand for certain supplies created unprecedented pressure on some supply chains. One of the more noticeable shifts in demand during the pandemic was the shift away from restaurant meals to cooking at home. Interestingly, the shortages seen in supermarkets was not, in most cases, due to a lack of food in the supply chain, but due to the fact that the supply chain was set up to supply much of the food in institutional packaging for restaurants. At one point, some supermarkets started to repackage the flour received for in-store bakeries into smaller consumer-sized packages because supply chains could not keep up with the demand for consumer-packaged flour.

Even without a pandemic, it is difficult for supply chains to react quickly to large changes in demand. A sudden change in consumer preference can cause ripples in supply chains across the world. Unfortunately for supply chain managers, the demands of consumers are changing faster than ever, creating the need for fast, flexible supply chains.

Some organizations such as coffee producers sometimes get involved in the very earliest part of production by investing and controlling farming practices to ensure adequate supply. Due to the difficult growing conditions and small-farm ownership in some coffee-producing countries, coffee companies must invest in farm infrastructure, water supplies, and other necessities to keep production stable.[3]

Modern SCM involves using technology to manage resources at every stage of the production process. ERP systems are critical to managing supply chains. ERP systems are used for placing orders, tracking them, paying for them, receiving them, and then tracking the progress as those raw supplies are turned into a product.

Another consideration in modern supply chains is the shift to green, renewable, and humanely sourced supplies. If it is not complicated enough to secure a continuous supply of resources for a business, it is now important for organizations to pay attention to how the suppliers treat their employees and the environment. Companies from Apple to Gap regularly audit their suppliers to ensure that their suppliers are treating their employees humanely, and not doing anything to harm the environment. A few decades ago, this kind of involvement in the business of a supplier was unheard of, but it is a reality in today's supply chains.

Depending on where you work, you may be involved in projects that directly impact the organization's supply chain. Whether it is working on an ERP project, optimizing supplier contracting, or any number of potential touch points, SCM is one of the most important aspects of any organization.

Future of Operations—Digital

As mentioned earlier in the chapter, there is a new type of operations management that sprung up as a result of the transition companies are making to become digital enterprises. The digital transformation taking place puts digital operations at the heart of the organization. Digital operations, sometimes called DigitalOps, put the companies' processes and data at the heart of the operation. DigitalOps helps organizations become more agile by coordinating resources and systems across the company.

Application to Project and Program Managers

In the beginning of this chapter, I said operations management and project management are opposites. I still stand by that statement, but the reality is that both of these professional fields need each other and both fulfill critical missions within an organization. Operations management is about keeping an organization stable and secure. Projects are about introducing change.

Given the scope of operations management, there is a strong chance that at some point, you will manage a project that impacts some aspect of it. Understanding the basics of operations management will help you be a better program manager. Even better, incorporating principles of operations management such as the process design, risk management, and Deming wheel can improve our project management practice.

Additional Resources

Free lean textbook: https://open.umn.edu/opentextbooks/textbooks/
beyond-lean-simulation-in-practice-second-edition

Free risk management textbook: https://open.umn.edu/opentextbooks/
textbooks/risk-management-for-enterprises-and-individuals

CHAPTER 6

Marketing

Why Study Marketing?

At first glance, there does not appear to be a lot of overlap between marketing and project and program management. Marketing is perceived by some to be about selling (or overselling) products to people or firms that do not want them. The negative stigma of tele-marketers invasively calling us at mealtime doesn't help. Nor does the negative perception of multilevel marketing schemes. These all detract from marketing's real purpose.

When we look at the definition of marketing from the American Marketing Association (AMA), marketing is much more closely aligned to project and program management than imagined at first pass: "Marketing is the activity, set of institutions, and processes for creating, communicating, delivering, and exchanging offerings that have value for customers, clients, partners, and society at large".[1] Thus, we see that marketing is about communicating and delivering value—one of the primary goals of project and program management.

Marketing is a large field with many specialty areas, but there are a few concepts and tools that project and program managers can learn from and even adopt into their project management practice such as:

- The power of building brands (both your personal brand as well as developing a project brand)
- Managing perceptions
- Developing the right product that will deliver value to those who use it
- Promotion techniques to gain audience attention

One more reason to study marketing is that we should all be aware that the world around us is heavily influenced by marketers. When you walk down a grocery store aisle and choose one brand over another, it's because you have been influenced by marketers to do so. I had one marketing professor who told us that if we ever saw the floor of a grocery store endcap (the small space at the end of each line of shelving that everyone has to pass by while traversing the store), that we should kneel on the ground and kiss it because it is the most expensive property in the world. Companies pay exorbitant rates to place their products on those endcaps because that prominent placement ensures the product will stand out to customers. When I realized that my free will to choose what products I wanted was largely the culmination of years of marketing influence, I was both saddened and amazed at the power of marketing. All of us should be aware of these influences in our life and be aware that we have the ability to use these marketing tools for the benefit of the programs for which we work.

In the remaining sections of this chapter, we will delve into the parts of marketing that have application to our profession.

Understanding the Basics

Power of Brand

When you think of the world's most powerful brands, you may think about a product, a service, a logo, an experience, or a combination of any of these attributes. The truth is, a brand is a *perception*. It is intangible. The value of the brand is made up of individual perceptions of the product, service, and company. Brands attempt to reinforce positive attributes and show differentiation from other brands. Brand value is fluid, and each experience a person has with a brand can increase or decrease the perceived brand value. Thus, brands must be continually managed and maintained.

Brands are not confined to formal, commercial entities. The concept of a brand can be powerfully applied to the way individuals perceive ourselves and our work. What kind of professional brand have you developed in your organization? What do people think of when your name is brought up? When you are assigned to a new project, what do leaders expect you will deliver? This is your personal brand and in the same way an organization nurtures its brand in the marketplace, you should manage your brand in the workplace.

Brand management encompasses the following key areas:

Define a Brand

When developing a brand, the most important consideration is defining the values it will represent and the value proposition it offers. What makes your product or service unique? Why would someone patronize your company versus a competitor? It is critical to clearly define what differentiates your product or service, and build your brand around that differentiation. Depending on what the differentiation is, you may want to appeal to cutting-edge, modern sensibilities, or to nostalgic, old-fashioned notions. You may want to project strength, or foster an aura of sensitivity. The attributes you can embrace in your brand are as endless as the strengths an organization (or individual) can have.

As a project and program manager, developing and nurturing a personal brand can boost you career. Think about your inherent strengths and weaknesses and think about how you can play to your strengths. If you are an exceptional scheduler or risk manager, find ways to bolster that perception in your organization so that when time-sensitive or high-risk programs come along, leadership immediately thinks about giving the project to you. Conversely, if you have had challenges delivering projects on time, or keeping the scope under control, you should think about how you can change perceptions about your ability to perform in those areas. Of course, you should not work on changing perceptions if those are legitimate areas of weakness. First, seek to improve your skills, then work on re-building your brand. If you work on brand perception first you will inevitably have problems again and could potentially lose your ability to fix those negative brand perceptions in the future.

Understand Competitive Landscape

Except for monopolies and government agencies, organizations exist in a competitive landscape. Organizations must understand what the competitive landscape is like to compete effectively. Is the marketplace packed with many low-cost competitors? Are the barriers to entry high or low? Which company is doing the most innovating? Which has the best customer experience? Knowing the way your brand is perceived in relation to competitors is essential to finding the most effective way to compete. If your brand is focused on customer experience, it is important to know which of your competitors also place value on customers, and which do not. This will allow you to hone your marketing and advertising to accentuate your competitive advantages and minimize areas of weakness.

Develop Consistency

Due to the fluid nature of brand perception, it is essential that an organization deliver on their value proposition consistently. With modern feedback mechanisms available on our phones at all times of the day, a customer can call out bad experiences quickly and viciously. A brand promise that is broken will, at a minimum, reduce brand value with the affected customer, and at worst, be broadcast across a vibrant social network, thus diminishing the brand universally. Loss of reputation is harder to fix than establishing a new brand reputation. It will take multiple positive experiences with the brand to regain the loss from one negative experience.

The same principles of consistency apply to our personal and professional brands. As a project and program manager you can successfully deliver many projects, but the first project with problems can impact your brand, especially if the problems are severe or highly visible. Gratefully, not all managers blame the project or program manager for a single project that go awry, but if a project manager develops a reputation for not delivering on time or on budget, their brand value may plummet, and they may end up looking for work elsewhere.

Measure Brand Value

Professional marketing leaders regularly assess the value of the brands under their control. This brand assessment can include surveys of buyers and likely buyers, focus groups, and comprehensive searches for the brand in all types of media. Brands that have worldwide recognition have astounding value. Products such as Coca Cola have brands worth tens of billions of dollars. In fact, in 2020, Coca Cola was considered the most valuable brand in the world with a value of $84B.[2]

It is important to realize that diversity in skill and ability is valuable to an organization, so strong personal brands that are different, but complimentary, should be a goal. Personal brands should not be used to compare yourself or others in ways that are negative. Celebrate each other's strengths and the diversity that naturally occurs in teams.

Perception

The word *perception* is used frequently when discussing marketing. In fact, marketing is built on perception. At the beginning of this chapter, I stated that brand is perception. The truth is, marketing is focused on understanding, building, and changing the perceptions of individuals and groups for the benefit of the organization they represent. A cynic might go so far as to say the purpose of marketing is to manipulate perception in others. *Forbes* magazine summarizes it well:

> *The perceptions consumers have of a brand, its values and its products and services can have a dramatic impact on consumer purchase behavior. If a business can foster positive perceptions focused on these aspects, it's likely to build a sustainable, loyal and growing customer base.*[3]

One of the key tools in a marketer's toolkit is a perceptual map. Perceptual maps plot the way a product and its competitors compare against each other. It uses two key attributes that are relevant to the product for the comparison. For example, if we do a perceptual map for our cupcake bakery, we might want to compare how people perceive the price and flavor of our cupcakes with those of our competition. A perception map may show that our cupcakes are perceived as expensive in the mind of potential customers, but that their flavor is superior. See Figure 6.1 for a sample perception map.

The kind of information in this perception map is enormously valuable to a marketer. Observations we can glean from this perception map include:

- Most bakeries price their cupcakes lower than we do.
- While most bakeries do not produce cupcakes with as much perceived flavor, there are a few that do. We need to watch out for Cosmo's Cakes.

Cupcake Bakery Perception Map

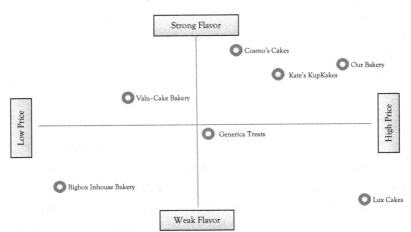

Figure 6.1 Sample perception map

- Our fiercest competitors will likely be those delivering the same amount of flavor at a lower cost. Again, Cosmo's Cakes could be a trouble for us because they are delivering a more flavorful product at a lower cost. We should also watch Kate's KupKakes because their cupcakes are perceived similarly to ours.
- Bakeries such as Lux Cakes probably won't be around long, unless there is another competitive factor at work.

Of course, there are other factors that could to be studied such as location, quality, or convenience in ordering that will help the bakery know how to compete, but it should be clear that perception maps are a powerfully simple way to show perception across key product or brand characteristics.

The Four Ps

The four key elements a marketer must consider when preparing a product to compete in the marketplace all happen to start with the letter *P*; thus, it is common to refer to these marketing elements as the *four Ps*. These four elements, product, promotion, price, and place, define the way a product shows up in the marketplace.

Product

Product is the actual product(s) or service(s) your organization sells. This is the most important thing your organization does and is the revenue-generating engine for the organization. The product should be aligned to the organization's vision and mission and should be driven by the brand image being built.

Promotion

Promotion is the way a product is advertised and boosted in the marketplace. Promotion can run the gamut from the corny "As Seen on TV" infomercials, to highly individualized target marketing efforts. It can include activities such as providing samples, placing ads, and sending catalogs. In addition to advertising, promotion can include public relations (PR) activities such as company announcements, placement of stories in the papers, and responses to crises or negative events.

Promotional activities should convey and support the overall brand strategy and messaging. For example, it would not be consistent for a luxury brand to use low-end promotional activities such as deep discounting, telemarketing, or stunt tactics. Every element of the marketing strategy should reinforce the overall perception of the brand and product in the mind of the buyer.

One of the more interesting tactics a marketer can use is when they do not advertise an actual product or service, but the company itself. There are times when a marketer may need to adjust public perception of the company independent of its products, meaning the promotion does not attempt to *sell* anything, except perception.

One of the major changes to promotion activities in the last couple of decades has been the transition of promotional efforts online. Now, promotion and placement can take place entirely in the digital space and may include developing relationships with influencers.

Pricing

While the price of a product or service seems like one of the most straightforward marketing elements, it is actually one of the most complex. Price is what the producer is willing to sell its product or service for, but price is also much more. Perceived value is a scale. It starts with commodity items at the bottom, and luxury items at the top, with many stops in between. Price communicates where on the scale producers want their product to be perceived.

When considering price, the seller has to consider more than just the cost to produce the service. You may be able to build the best television in the world, but if it costs you a million dollars to do it, you cannot expect the television will find many customers because there are many great options at a lower price point. When pricing your good or service, you must consider what the market is willing to pay for it.

Charging What the Market Will Bear

Sometimes what a buyer is willing to pay can work to a provider's favor. Early in my career, I had to lay off an employee who had a specialized, but obsolete skillset. The company developed software on multiple computer platforms, including VAX/VMS, a computer, and an operating system developed by DEC Corporation in the 1970s. We had turned off most of the VAX units, except for one we kept alive for legacy support purposes. It was decided that we'd accept the risk (remember the section on risk) of letting our last VAX/VMS administrator go because there was only one unit left to manage. While it was an intense experience to lay someone off (it was my first time), it was also intense when the unit failed and management decided we needed to bring it back online. After looking at options, we decided to call this former employee and ask if he would be willing to come in for a few hours to diagnose and repair the unit. Gratefully, he was willing, but he knew that if we were calling him, that it must be important, and his quoted rate for the repair was astronomical. Ultimately, we were willing to pay him his requested fee because it was worth it to the company, and the employee knew it.

There are stories of luxury manufacturers who increased prices and subsequently saw *more* sales because it triggered a greater luxury perception. This happens more when it is harder for a consumer to judge the value of the product or service. In those cases, the consumer will sometimes use price as a way to judge quality.[4] Thus, the higher the price, the more perceived quality, and the more the product or service may sell.

Other considerations in pricing are whether discounting is appropriate, and if so, how to do it. Some companies seem to engage in an *always on sale* strategy, with regular discounts available. Others rarely or never discount their products. The discounting strategy you employ is a strong signal to the market about your brand. As you can imagine, those products that rarely provide discounts are typically in upscale markets.

Finally, another consideration is how the products are sold. Are the products available on the Internet? Is there a network of dealers or partners who sell for you? Do you have a team of sales people on payroll to do the selling for you? The type of product may dictate the model used, but on occasion, the models are broken by newcomers. For example, when Elon Musk brought his Tesla electric cars to market, he chose not to use a dealership model and instead sell cars directly to consumers. This was actually illegal in some states, and Tesla has had to work with regulators to make his approach possible. By cutting out dealers, Tesla is able to capture more of the profits, but the company also has to manage all the promotions, contracts, and delivery to consumers, which dealers would normally take care of for the manufacturer.

While there are myriad ways to price a product or service, there are several tried-and-true approaches:

Cost-Plus Pricing

An organization that uses cost-plus pricing carefully examines what the production of the product or service costs them, then adds a standard percentage to that cost to derive their price. It is common for retail organizations to use this kind of pricing and simply mark-up the cost of goods by a standard percentage. The advantage to this pricing model is that it is straightforward and easy to implement and understand. A major downside is that it completely ignores what the market is willing to pay for the goods or services.

Competitive-Based Pricing

Some organizations use the prices charged by their competitors to set the price for their product or service. Gas stations that are on the same corner sometimes use this method to price their gasoline. At first, this can cause prices to drop, as one station may price slightly less than the other, and then, each station responds in kind. But eventually, an equilibrium is found. Sometimes, one of the competitors will intentionally move their price up in hopes the others will follow suit. Airlines use this method when they are in especially brutal price-cutting cycles. One airline will try to signal to the others that it's mutually destructive to keep price cutting by upping their prices, but if other airlines don't respond, this increased price will not last long, as they will cut costs again to avoid losing business. As long as companies signal in the market they intend to move up prices (as opposed to a meeting), it is allowable. If competing companies knowingly plan to keep prices high, it can be *collusion*, and is illegal because it harms the consumer.

The downsides of competitive-based pricing are the opposite of cost-plus methods because competitive pricing pays no attention to the internal costs to create the cost or service. In the case of the airlines, it can create scenarios where airlines will sell seats at prices that are below their costs, which is unsustainable.

Value-Based Selling

Value-based selling is about selling to the customer at the value the customer is willing to pay. This kind of costing does not work in a commodity market where prices are well established. In large enterprise software deals, it is not uncommon for the price charged to one customer to vary quite a bit from another. This is because the details of these deals are often private, and because these transactions don't take place often, there is not a widely publicized price for the software or services. This allows the salesperson latitude in what to charge the customer. The idea is that the customer will pay at the rate they value for the product or service.

Price Skimming

Price skimming is a strategy where a provider initially prices higher, then as time passes, they drop the price, often multiple times. The strength of this kind of pricing strategy can be seen in a simple supply and demand chart. By using a skimming strategy, the producer is able to gather sales at all parts of the demand curve.

Price skimming can also take advantage of the fact that the cost to produce products and services often decreases with volume and time.

Penetration Pricing

When a company has a new, large market opportunity it can tap into, it may be wise to grab as many customers as possible even if the company loses money at first. This is a common practice for high-tech startup companies. These startups knowingly sell their products at a price point where the company is losing money knowing that once the company has strong market penetration, it can start to raise the price it charges customers and, thus, turn the company profitable. This model is only possible if the company has abundant financial resources or has backers that understand the model and are willing to invest and wait until it becomes profitable.

Penetration pricing, like price skimming, takes advantage of all aspects of the economic demand curve; it just does so in a different way.

Place

Place is the location and manner an organization chooses to sell its products or services. As discussed in the preceding pricing section, the place can be on the Internet, on the shelf of a store, through a team of sales people or through a network of partners. The overriding principles marketing professionals consider with place is getting the product as close to the customer as possible to make it easy for them to purchase. The type of product or service you deliver will help dictate the place.

Other Marketing Responsibilities

Public Relations

My undergraduate degree is in PR. I had dreams of managing relationships with media, representing companies on television news, and handling crises with the media. While I abandoned the dream before I ever actually took a job in the field, I have remembered many of the key principles of the field.

PR is a key part of the team that manages the way the company shows up in the media. Companies can show up in the media in a positive or negative way. Managing negative stories is sometimes called crisis management, and there are tried-and-true playbooks PR teams can use when they are caught in a crisis.

One of the more interesting roles PR plays is in the placement of positive stories. You may be surprised to learn that PR professionals outnumber journalists nearly 6:1.[5] Some estimates put the amount of news stories prompted by PR activity at greater than 50 percent. With this massive amount of influence PR practitioners have, it is essential that organizations have their own advocates to ensure the news is portraying the organization and its market offerings in the best light possible.

Advertising

Advertising is similar to PR, in that it uses media to tell the company's story, but advertising is a paid transaction rather than news reporting. Advertising is such a large and important component within business that companies such as Google built their business model on the sale of advertising.

Advertising is a key component to transmitting brand messaging. The way a company chooses to advertise signals a lot about a brand. If they choose to put full-color, back-cover advertisements in influential magazines, it signals something different than a small classified ad in the back of a newspaper. If that example is too old school, gaining the endorsement of a top influencer is different than a pop-up ad on a website. Sometimes, in advertising, less is more, meaning that a few well-placed ads are more powerful than a full-on, in your face, advertising blitz. Top products do not need a lot of advertising because word of mouth and reputation are doing much of the advertising on their behalf.

In the next section, we will take a brief look at digital marketing, including the roles of social media in marketing.

Digital Marketing

The advent of the Internet also ushered in an all-new way to reach potential customers. Marketers recognized and adapted to these changes, and digital marketing was born. Digital marketing encompasses all the ways buyers can be reached online. Digital marketers work hard to ensure their products and services rank high in search engines, that advertisements are seen on websites and mobile devices, that their names are mentioned by social media influencers, and that reputations are managed on product and service rating services. Depending on the product or service, the only marketing done may be in the digital realm. The experience each of us has when on the Internet or our mobile devices has been heavily influenced (some would say manipulated) by for-profit organizations packed with digital marketing experts.

Search Engine Marketing

Since the start of digital marketing, the importance of search engine advertising has grown significantly. In the early 1990s, as the Internet was gaining popularity, and search engines, as we know them, today did not exist. Sites such as Yahoo! came online as Web directories, which were giant indexes of nested links that attempted to provide visitors a way to access all corners of the Internet. As websites multiplied, the Web directory model was straining and eventually Web search engines offered a new way to find what you needed on the Internet.

Marketers soon realized that the way results were returned was important. Marketers developed two ways to influence where their products and services show up in the results. First, they use free techniques such as optimizing content, using searchable keywords, and adding meta data. This kind of effort is often called search engine optimization (SEO). Marketers can also pay for preferred placement in search engines. Search engines charge for better placement, and those websites, products, and services in the first few results received far more response than those ranked lower. This kind of effort is often called search engine marketing (SEM).

Device/Mobile Marketing

Approximately half of the Internet viewing that takes place is done on mobile devices.[6] This means that smart marketers will be looking at ways to make the mobile experience work best for their product placement activities.

Mobile marketing takes many forms. *In-app* marketing may be one of the most significant areas because nearly 88 percent of all screen time on mobile devices is within applications.[7] This does not mean that to market your product or service, you need to build an app. Digital advertising platforms allow relevant ads to surface on a consumer device. The trick is making sure the information you choose to convey is suited to a mobile audience. You have just seconds to communicate your message before the consumer is looking at other things.

Other mobile marketing techniques include in-game marketing, QR codes, text messaging, and more.

Web Properties

At the beginning of the Internet age, this would have been called *building a website*, but the many ways of reaching consumers digitally have made the idea of a website-only strategy quaint. With social media platforms such as Instagram, Facebook, Twitter, TikTok, and others, an organization must think more broadly about how to reach potential customers. Just as a person might build a portfolio of real estate properties, smart marketers will build a portfolio of websites, social media pages, and social media accounts to broaden their reach. When done right, each Web property builds and reinforces the other, creating great customer involvement and stickiness.

Social Media

As referenced in the preceding section, acquiring and maintaining appropriate Web properties are critical to reaching potential customers. Social media takes that idea to new levels by allowing interaction with the customer outside of the actual purchase transaction. Even more recently, the expectation that people's favorite brands take a stand on political issues has made social media an even more important platform for signaling brand affiliation with causes. Roles such as social media manager did not exist 20 years ago, but jobs such as these are now some of the most visible roles in an organization.

Reputation Management

As organizations embrace social media and other digital marketing platforms, it is natural that things will sometimes go wrong. Bad user reviews, significant service outages, executive scandals, and other events can create a negative reputation for an organization. Managing the organization's reputation is an ongoing activity, but during a crisis, it can become an organizational imperative. Consulting teams have sprung up to help organizations manage their online reputations.

Application to Project and Program Management

As stated at the beginning of this chapter, experienced project and program managers will learn from and apply core marketing principles to help them manage their careers and personal brands. Learning to manage perceptions within an organization will help you manage your projects in an elevated way. As you work through projects that impact a lot of people, managing the way critical project messaging takes place can help your project go from good to great.

I encourage you to think about and augment your personal brand by participating in professional enrichment activities such as training and conferences. I also encourage you to consider ways to get involved in local and regional project management professional groups. Take on leadership roles, develop presentations, participate in networking events, write articles for project management publications—all of these activities will allow you to augment and extend your personal brand with like-minded colleagues. You will, in effect, be marketing yourself as a first-class project and program manager.

At the organizational level, marketing teams are highly active and fast moving. In my experience, they also spawn a lot of projects. It is possible you may manage a marketing-focused project at some point in your career, so understanding the basics of marketing is important.

Additional Resources

Free marketing textbook: https://open.umn.edu/opentextbooks/textbooks/
    introducing-marketing
Free marketing textbook: https://open.umn.edu/opentextbooks/textbooks/
    principles-of-marketing

CHAPTER 7

Entrepreneurship

Why Study Entrepreneurship?

One of the reasons I chose to go to business school was to see if I had the right skills and emotional constitution to start my own business. I had ideas for starting my own company, but at that point in my life, I didn't have the courage to strike out on my own. I felt that business school would give me the skills to take my idea to fruition while also being an environment where I could test the other skills required for success.

I am not alone in having ambitions to start my own business. A 2018 study of MBA applicants[1] asked prospects where they saw themselves in 10 years. The results showed that more than 60 percent saw themselves running their own company, the number one response to this question. MBA programs understand this, and most reputable programs have entrepreneurship as a specialization you can pursue.

It turns out that I learned valuable entrepreneurial skills, but more importantly, I got the clarification I needed that I was not, at that time, ready to be an entrepreneur. I estimate learning that lesson saved me from years of frustration and financial hardship.

What does this have to do with becoming a better program manager? At a minimum, it will help you understand the motivations, worries, and needs of leadership in your organization as they attempt to build a successful organization. At its best, learning about entrepreneurship could help you marry your existing program management skills to those of successful entrepreneurs, creating a powerful combination of organization and vision. Many of the attributes that make people great project and program managers translate to entrepreneurship.

Understanding the Basics

Like any profession, entrepreneurs come in many shapes and sizes—but thanks to business programs, the most important skills needed to be successful have been identified, studied, and packaged into learning modules. It is important to call out that starting and running any kind of business makes you entrepreneurial—but starting and running a small corner bakery is vastly different than founding a successful high-tech, biotech, or industrial company. If you want to start a small retail establishment, there are literally hundreds of franchise opportunities that will guide you step-by-step in how to get started. While there is an overlap of skills required, a good business school will prepare you to identify large market opportunities, create a credible business plan, find financing for your venture, and really leave your mark on the world. This will be covered more in the section *Are You Really an Entrepreneur?* For now, know that the topics and skills discussed in the following section are more suited for larger entrepreneurial pursuits than a mom-and-pop sandwich shop.

Identifying Opportunities

There are two primary considerations in identifying opportunities. The first is finding ideas that interest you. The second is finding ideas that *will actually be successful.* Think of the process like a funnel. A person could develop literally thousands of new ideas on which to base a new business. The entrepreneur needs to dump all of those ideas into the top of the funnel and have only the most viable opportunities come out at the bottom. We will examine both ends of the funnel in the next section.

New Business Ideation

New business ideas can come from almost anywhere, but the majority of ideas can be sorted into standard categories outlined as follows.

Correcting a Market Inefficiency

Markets are inefficient when the products or services are under- or over-valued by the marketplace. This can happen when the market is not willing to pay for a product or service at a price level a company can sustain. The reverse can happen, and the demand can spike, and a company cannot keep up with demand. Where there is market inefficiency, there is opportunity to remedy the issue and profit as a result. If you can find ways to lower the manufacturing cost of a previously overpriced product, you might have a success on your hands.

Bringing Existing Products or Services to New Markets

Do you have a favorite product or service in your area that does not exist in other markets? Or have you visited a new place and discovered something you wish you could take back home with you? You may have an entrepreneurial opportunity in front of you. These kinds of experiences happen frequently, and market forces are such that these kinds of opportunities can be quite fleeting as new trends, products, and services spread across the world.

Bringing New Products or Services to Market

Creating a new product or service and bringing it to market is often what people think of when they think of starting a new company. Dating back hundreds of years, people try to *invent* something new the world just cannot live without. While one of the more traditional ways of thinking about entrepreneurship, it can also be one of the most difficult to manage because it can involve not just creating the product or service, but also the market for it.

Bringing New or Improved Versions of Existing Products to Market

This is also a common way to create a new business. If a product in the marketplace can be improved in some way that jumpstarts demand, it can open a significant market opportunity. Improvements can take the form of new functionality, better delivery, improved value, or many other factors. Some examples include, Uber improving on taxis, and front loader washing machines improving on top loaders.

Scientific Breakthrough

Applied research, drug discovery, weapons research, and other fields are continually developing scientific breakthroughs that can sometimes be applied to commercial markets. Some U.S. national laboratories have commercialization offices that work with external parties to gain access to their scientific breakthroughs. Many very successful companies have been built on scientific breakthrough.

Change in Government Regulation

Changes made by federal, state, and local governments can be a treasure trove of commercial opportunity for those who are prepared to capitalize on the change. Think about the Covid-19 pandemic and state and local face mask orders. An entire industry was spawned by the new regulation. Sometimes, subtle changes in rules can have sweeping impacts on commercial markets.

Finding the Right Opportunities

With the top of the opportunity funnel covered, we will now turn our attention to the bottom of the funnel, and specifically, the screening criteria to ensure that only the best ideas make it out.

Size of the Opportunity

The most interesting idea may not be the best one if the total addressable market is limited. To catch the attention of investors, an opportunity must be quite significant. Anything less than $10M per year may be considered a *lifestyle* business—not one worthy of outside investment. Investors look for opportunities that are often in the hundreds of millions of dollars for the company, and the company will only be expected to own a portion of the overall market, meaning the addressable market may need to be $1B or greater before it is interesting. As you look at potential business ideas, be sure you are scoping them correctly for your business vision.

Margins/Profitability

Expected profit margins vary by industry and capital structure, but need to be sufficient so that they provide benefits to all steps of the sales channel. It is not uncommon for a company to need to sell a product that costs $10 to manufacture for $50 or more in the marketplace because cost structures demand it. As you consider ideas for a business, be sure the product is fundamentally profitable from the start. Profit margin erodes over time due to market pressure, making initial profitability critical.

Competition

The competitive landscape of your new venture is critical to its long-term viability. Using the Covid-19 face mask example from earlier in the chapter, the competition in the first few months was limited, and the first companies to bring masks to the marketplace in bulk were likely quite profitable, but because of the large overall business opportunity, many companies were lured into the market, and in time, an abundance of non-medical masks became available. It is important to look at long-term competitive forces when possible.

Defending Your Moat

Products and services that have a solid barrier to entry should be prioritized over those that do not. If it is easy to enter a market, there will naturally be more competition and more pressure on profit margins. If barriers to entry are high, you will have a better chance of defending and controlling the market if you can break in. Barriers to entry can include substantial startup costs, patents, exclusive access to components, expertise, and other factors. The more of these you have, the larger the moat you can build to protect your market and margins.

Passion for the Idea

Finally, anyone who starts down the entrepreneurial path will want to be passionate about the idea they are pursuing because they will be living and breathing all aspects of the idea for years to come. Even the best idea to come out of the idea funnel will not be successful if the entrepreneur is unable to muster excitement for it.

Business Models and Planning

Once you have your idea, you will need to consider two things: your business model and your business plan. Both of these will be explained in subsequent sections.

Business Models

Business models define the fundamental way your business interacts with the market place and generates its revenue. Will you sell directly to businesses through a team of salespeople or through a channel of value-added resellers? Or will you sell to consumers directly (e-commerce), or through retail outlets (Best Buy, Target, etc.)? Or will you focus on government sales, multilevel marketing, app stores, or some other method? Will you give away a free or trial version to hook people on your product? These decisions are fundamental to the way you will set up your business, develop your business plan, and ultimately run your business.

There are dozens of legitimate business models in use, and new models are regularly developed. We will look at four major business models in Table 7.1 as a starting point for you to think through your business idea.

As stated earlier, these are very broad business models. The key is to think carefully about who you are actually selling your product to and create your organization to support those sales. Once you have your business model figured out, it is time to develop your business plan.

Business Plans

A business plan details many important decisions around how your business will be run. It will detail what your company is about, what market it is selling into, what competitive advantages your business has, projected (pro-forma) financial estimates for three to five years, how you will market and sell your products or services, how much funding you will need to make all of this happen, and how long it will take.

As a project and program manager, you may find creating a business plan similar to creating a project plan. There certainly are similarities, but you must think of a business plan as a marketing document more than an execution plan. The purpose of a business plan is to attract executives and

Table 7.1 Common business models

Business models	Description
Business-to-consumer (B2C)	This is a familiar model to most of us. When you walk into a department store, order from an online site, or purchase groceries, you are participating in a B2C transaction as the consumer. These business models rely on thousands (or millions) of small transactions for their revenue. These transactions can be in person, online, from a catalog, over the phone, or in other creative ways. Businesses that sell to consumers must pay attention to consumer trends, macro-economic trends, and other forces to ensure their offerings are as appealing as possible to the largest possible group of consumers.
Business-to-business (B2B)	When one business sells products or services to another business, it is engaged in B2B transactions. These transactions are vastly different from B2C transactions because these purchases can often be very large. I worked for a software company that had a sales cycle that averaged more than a year, meaning that the company would not expect to sell anything to a prospective company for more than a year after initial contact from a sale representative. The upside is the deals could often be valued into the tens of millions. Of course, not all B2B transactions are so drawn out, but the way a company sells to another business is very different and needs to be accounted for in your business plan.
Consumer-to-consumer (C2C)	C2C sales have existed for hundreds of years with bartering, flea markets, and other person-to-person sales mechanisms. How can a business model be built on these kinds of transactions? Ask eBay! They created a marketplace to facilitate C2C transactions and skim their revenue from each transaction.
Consumer-to-business (C2B)	The C2B model can be a little harder to understand. It is when an individual sells to a business. But when is this done? Businesses such as Upwork created a marketplace for individuals to sell services to business; this is a great example of C2B in action.

employees, investors, customers, and other supporters to your vision. This means that, while accuracy is an important goal, it is equally important to create excitement about the opportunity you are presenting.

There are hundreds of business plan templates in circulation. Some are good, and many are really bad. You will need to search through what is available and make a decision for what is right for you. As there are so many ways to create a business plan, it is recommended that you read the business plans of other businesses. To do this, start to network with other entrepreneurs and ask to see their plans. Much can be learned by reading other plans. Be sure to ask whether the plan was used to seek a business loan or other financing. If a business plan has been successfully used to gain investments from outsiders, it is going to be better than most. Don't be surprised if the business plan only loosely resembles the business in real life. A plan rarely comes to life as written. If you take the entrepreneur's path, you will need to trust the plan, but pivot from it as opportunities and roadblocks surface.

Financing Your Venture

The best funding option is to self-fund your venture. You retain full control of the company, and the financial upside is enormous. Of course, the risk is all yours as well when you self-fund. The problem is most people don't have funds to start a large venture on their own (or without risking personal assets like their home). Given this, we will look at two other funding options: taking out a business loan and seeking equity investments from third parties such as angel investors.

The fundamental difference between these two funding options is that loans introduce debt onto the balance sheet. The loan will need to be paid back, with interest, over time. When the loan is paid, there is no further involvement with the lender. Outside equity hits the balance sheet as an investment, and part of the company equity is given away. If you, as the founder, own 100 percent of the company at the start, and you issue equity to gain investment to grow the business, you must give up some of your ownership (and control). If you give away more than 50 percent of the company to gain the investment, you are no longer in control of the company, the other investor(s) are in control. We will examine the benefits and pitfalls of each option in subsequent sections.

It is also important to understand that investors in early-stage companies are making risky investments, and because of the risk they are assuming, they expect high returns. The younger the company, the riskier it is, and the more expensive getting funding will be. Once a company has a track record of either profits, or progress toward profitability, it will be less risky, and raising money will be less expensive in terms of ownership given away.

Business Loan

Business loans come in many shapes and sizes, but in the United States, a substantial number of business loans come through the Small Business Administration (SBA) loan program run by the federal government. Banks will make loans to entrepreneurs outside of this program, but the requirements for the loans will differ and likely be more stringent.

The SBA has many options depending on whether you are looking for a small business loan (up to $350,000), or up to $5M for larger ventures. The SBA does not actually issue the loan—banks issue the loans under the SBA program, so you will work directly with a bank. The benefits and challenges of using loans for funding are outlined as follows:

Benefits of using loans (debt):

- Maintain ownership and control of the business.
- Straight-forward application process through banks (especially under the SBA program).
- As long as you make your payment, the lender will not get involved in the operation of your business.
- No board of directors' seat will need to be given up for the funding.

Challenges of using loans (debt):

- You may need to use personal property (house, car, etc.) as collateral for the loan. If the business cannot repay the loan, you could lose your personal property.
- Having to make debt payments when a business is just getting started can create undue strain on the organization.
- Loan limits are generally low for creating a larger venture. Loans may be able to help at the very beginning, but business needs can quickly outstrip the ability to secure a large enough loan.

When starting your venture, a loan is a viable funding option, but be sure you consider the downsides of debt and the potential benefits of using equity financing instead.

Equity Funding

When people dream of starting their own business, it is common to dream about receiving a large cash infusion from a big-time venture capitalist (VC) and eventually listing the company on a stock exchange in an initial public offering (IPO). While this is a possibility, the reality is that equity funding comes in stages (called rounds) and from other sources than just VCs and IPOs. Each option has benefits and challenges, and entrepreneurs need to be aware of each when making funding decisions. All of these equity funding options depend on the way you set up your company (see the next section *Corporate Structures*). Equity financing depends on setting up a corporation versus a sole proprietorship or partnership.

Three important principles need to be understood when considering equity funding:

1. The percentage of the company you have to give away is dependent on the value of the company. For example, if the value of your company is $500,000, and you need to raise $100,000, then you will need to sell approximately 20 percent of the company to raise those funds. When you are in early stages and all you have so far is an idea and a plan, you have to give away a lot more equity because your company is not worth much at that point. Once you have your product nearly done and you have proven there is market demand, the value of your company is worth substantially more, so you can give away less ownership to others to get funding. Smart entrepreneurs are careful to control when and how much of their organization they give away to others on their way to success.

2. You need to establish the type of shares and the total number of shares you will divide your company into (and thus give away in exchange for funding). Whether you create your corporation with a thousand shares or a million shares doesn't really matter. What does matter is tracking who owns those shares and understanding the impact of issuing additional shares later, as this will dilute the ownership of those who have early shares. For example, say your company authorizes one million shares, and during your funding journey, you trade 400,000 shares for funding (40 percent

ownership) from outside investors. If you later need to raise additional funding, you could authorize the sale of an additional million shares, but the ownership of those original investors would be halved, because those 400,000 shares are now only 20 percent of the total number of shares issued. Some early investors understand this is a possibility and may ask for an anti-dilution clause in their contract, which can create its own issues.

3. Issuing and selling equity is highly regulated by government entities because of the strong potential for fraud. Unscrupulous business people can easily bilk unsophisticated investors with grand promises that simply cannot be backed up, causing complete loss of investment. Be careful as you make plans to issue equity that you are in full compliance with local and federal laws.

Funding From Individuals

One of the most common sources of equity funding, especially very early on, is friends and family. Parents or other family that believe in you and your idea may agree to give you funding in exchange for partial ownership in your company. While this kind of support can be appreciated, funding at this stage has some downsides:

- Taking money from family and friends can strain personal relationships. Sitting down to dinner with family and friends feels different when there is a business transaction in place, especially when business is not going well.
- The percentage of the company you have to give away early on is greater than when the company is more established. A small early investment may give a family member or friend a sizeable ownership and influence for years to come.

Funding From Angel Investors

Entrepreneurs often find that initial funding from friends and family is helpful, but not sufficient enough to grow their company into a larger venture. The problem is, they are still too small to be attractive to VCs who typically fund organizations that are more established and growing rapidly. What is an entrepreneur to do? Thankfully, angel investors are an investor class that has stepped in to bridge the gap. These are often high net-worth individuals (or small groups) who have set aside funds to invest in promising young companies. These investors are looking for high returns because they are assuming a lot of risk by investing in an early stage company.

Angel investors are more sophisticated investors than family and friends and will, therefore, expect to see substantial evidence your company will be successful. These investors typically have specific industry experience and may want to invest in young companies in their areas of expertise. If they believe in your company, they may help in ways that are more than financial. They may be able to open doors with suppliers, customers, and even other investors. Typically, they do not want direct involvement in the running of the company but will expect regular updates on company progress. As angel investors are more sophisticated, be sure you have your plans clearly developed and understand the value of your company at this stage. You also need to have a clear plan for how these investors will be getting their money back from you. Having ownership in a company that is not publicly traded makes cashing out of an investment more difficult. This is why, many companies seek an IPO, so all the investors from the earlier stage have an avenue to collect their returns. Another common plan is to seek acquisition by a larger organization. This may also allow early investors to get out of their original investment.

Funding From Venture Capitalists

Growing companies love to share when they get a new round of funding from VCs. The more prominent the VC group, the better the bragging rights. But getting funding from a VC group is not easy, and it comes with many strings attached. VCs are in business to make money. They will not view your company as a work of passion, but in cold, hard financial terms. They will take substantial equity for their investment, and likely a place (or two or three) on your board of directors. They want to strongly influence the direction of the company to ensure the success of their investment. But it's not all bad because they will often bring industry expertise, CEO mentorship, and other critical tools to help the company be successful. This is also the critical time when your own leadership will be tested.

If you are starting a business and expect to stay on as CEO for many years, you will need to prove that you can run the company as well as a seasoned CEO from the industry. VCs may insist that the company founder(s) step aside from the day-to-day running of the company in exchange for their investment. This can be a big blow to a founder's ego, but is likely the right move for the company. The skills it takes to start a company are not the same it takes to run a larger organization. It is a rare person who can run a company at all stages of its development.

Funding from VCs comes in rounds that are usually labeled as Series A, Series B, and so on. Series A funding is the earliest stage a VC firm will engage with a company. Each additional round of funding represents a step in the company's maturity. If you are fortunate enough to be negotiating with a VC firm, be sure to talk to others who have used that VC to ensure the company's approach is right for you.

What Is the Difference Between Venture Capital and Private Equity?

Sometimes terms like venture capital and private equity are thrown around loosely, blurring the lines between what they do. But each of them is targeting different investment types, and it is good to know the differences between funding sources. Venture capital companies target smaller companies with great potential. Private equity companies often target broken companies that, with some rehabilitation, can become great once again. Private equity companies often take public companies and make them private again. This allows them to make more substantial changes in the operation of the company, and then they take the company public again so they can get their investment payoff. Private equity companies do not invest in early-stage companies, and you will not work with them on growing your company.

Exit Strategies

Earlier in this chapter, I introduced the idea that investors are going to want to know when and how they will get their payoff. Understanding possible exit strategies is important because your business plan will need to include a major *equity event* such as IPO or acquisition.

Initial Public Offering

When a company is *private*, they are able to operate with less rules and oversight. They are also hampered in their ability to reach investors because there is not a clear way for them to get their money out of the investment. The trade-off is that publicly traded companies give you an exit strategy but they must follow extensive financial reporting rules. These rules require a lot of overhead, so companies must be of sufficient size for it to make sense to go public. A small company would be crushed under the reporting requirements.

If you are at the point you are ready to go public, you will have acquired a team of investors who are vested in helping you get through an IPO. You will need to find an investment firm to underwrite (sell) your stock offering, attorneys to develop your prospectus, and a team of other advisors that will all take a sizeable chunk of money to retain. IPOs are not cheap to do, but the rewards can make founders millionaires (or more!).

But not all IPOs make a big splash in the marketplace. I once worked for a small company that wanted access to public markets, but was too small for a major IPO. Leadership chose to trade on the over-the-counter (OTC) market, which is a less-prestigious marketplace for small companies that want to be public. Once the decision was made to go public, much of our attention turned from product development to preparing the prospectus. I recall hours of work going in to just one paragraph of the prospectus because each word you write will be scrutinized by potential investors and could become a point of contention in court, should investments not pay off. As sometimes happens, before we actually went public, another company offered to buy the company.

In the next section, we will learn about the other equity event that early investors look forward to if an IPO is not in the works.

Acquisition

While IPOs tend to be sexier and have more excitement around them, selling your company to a larger company is a very respectable exit strategy that can be more straightforward for the founder. The outcome of selling will be either (or both) cash for your shares, or new shares in the acquiring company. While cash is best, if the acquiring company is public, there is at least an avenue for getting your money.

Important considerations for acquisition:

1. You will need to negotiate your role (if any) in the combined company. Some purchasers will want to keep the founder onboard for a period of time to ensure a smooth transition, while others will want to be sure the founders are out of the picture so as to ensure there is no interference with their plans.

2. The acquiring firm may want to keep some of your employees, but not others. Your employees were instrumental in getting you to the point of acquisition. It is the right thing to do to take care of your employees the best you can whenever an equity event happens. You will not be able to control what happens to your employees once the other firm takes over, so be sure they will benefit from the acquisition before it happens.

3. Acquisitions are sometimes all cash, but more often include some exchange of shares. The number of shares your company is worth in comparison to the shares of the acquiring company is a critical negotiating point. As with IPOs, it's recommended you surround yourself with trusted advisors who can help you steer your company through the selling process.

Corporate Structures

Some subjects are best left to true professionals. When it comes to making decisions about the type of legal structure your business should form, I strongly advise you to consult a good lawyer with experience in these matters. But as you think about how to legally set up your business, there are things you should consider based on your circumstance and based on the

outcome you want. If you are building a small business and don't antici-
pate needing outside investors, a simple entity such as a sole proprietorship or partnership may suffice. If you plan to seek outside investment,
you will need to form a legal entity called a corporation. There are many
types of corporations, each with benefits and challenges.

Protection From Risk

One of the biggest considerations when you form a new legal entity is
the protection it provides to the owner. For example, if you run a small
cupcake shop as an individual proprietor and you accidentally put in an
ingredient that causes an allergic reaction to a patron, you could be personally liable for any legal consequences. This means you could lose your
home, car, and any other assets as a result of activities of the business.
If that same cupcake shop was set up as a corporation, any legal consequences would stay within the corporation. You might lose your business,
but you would not lose your personal assets.

Ease of Getting Investors

The other big consideration of entity type is the ease with which you can
divide up ownership to bring in outside investors. Sole proprietorships and
partnerships are totally inappropriate for fundraising purposes of any meaningful size. You should seriously consider setting up a corporation to protect
yourself and your investors and make it easier to sell shares. Corporations
come with requirements, including formation and registration fees, but if you
are a serious entrepreneur, you will not think twice about forming a corporation. Even within the corporate world, there are different types of corporations with different attributes, so obtaining quality legal advice to determine
the right structure and file the right paperwork is important. General types of
legal entities in the United States are reviewed in subsequent sections.

Legal Entity Types

Limited Liability Corporation (LLC)

Limited liability corporation (LLC) structures are a relatively new type of
legal entity and are appropriate for smaller companies, or larger companies that don't plan to issue shares. The fundamental ownership element

of an LLC is a partner, not shares. This makes IPOs impossible. But because the LLC structure is less formal and has less requirements, it is a popular option for smaller companies. LLCs can be taxed as partnerships or as full corporations, depending on owner preference.

Corporation Type-S (S-Corp)

This type of corporation has more structure and requirements than an LLC, but is still less structured than a full corporate entity. These are popular with founders who are looking for tax advantages found in smaller organizations, but with the risk protection of a corporation. Unfortunately, S-Corps are not appropriate for any company that will eventually seek an IPO.

Corporation Type-C (C-Corp)

This is a full corporation, with shares being the basic ownership unit. This is the structure that nearly all larger companies will use. Forming and keeping a corporation in place can take money and time, but as an organization grows, this overhead becomes a minor consideration. C-Corps are taxed as separate entities (unlike LLCs and S-Corps, which can pass through taxes to individuals). Because C-Corps are taxed at an individual level, and then shareholders are taxed at a personal level, there is a perception that C-Corps are double-taxed.

Tax situation aside, this is likely the corporate entity to consider if you are planning to build a large corporation using equity investment.

Are You Really an Entrepreneur?

Now that you understand the basics of entrepreneurship, it is important to ask yourself whether or not you have the right skills and personality to be successful. Entrepreneurship is often glamorized in the media, but what is not shown are the countless hours of time you put in to ensure the company's success, or the regular rejection you face when selling your idea to others. Entrepreneurs have to be a mix of contradictions. They need to be resilient while being able to take constructive criticism. They need to be visionary while being able to plan and organize. They need to be able to sell their ideas to others while maintaining optimism about their ability to succeed.

Considerations for Project and Program Managers

I said at the beginning of this chapter that there are a lot of qualities that project and program managers share with entrepreneurs. This is true, but there are other skills an entrepreneur must have that are not always in a program manager's toolkit. I will call out some of the more important considerations you need to make before starting down the entrepreneurship path.

Flexibility

I find that the best project and program managers tend to be very organized. This is a great quality for an entrepreneur as long as it is tempered with the ability to be flexible and pivot quickly when circumstances change. When agile practices started to make their way into traditional project management, I witnessed a divide between people who wanted to embrace the new methodology and those who would not. A person cannot be a good entrepreneur if they are unable to be flexible and change direction when a newer or better option presents itself. Flexibility is also a quality that strong project and program managers foster because changes to projects are inevitable, and you need to flex with those changes.

Risk Tolerance

Good project and program managers are well trained in managing risk. We are taught to catalog, measure, and report risk as part of our stewardship. However, the risk we almost always talk about in project management is *negative* risk, or downside risk. These are risks that can keep us from getting to our goal. When starting a venture, an entrepreneur must be able to tolerate a great amount of negative risk because they are seeking to pursue the flipside of negative risk, sometimes called opportunity. A program manager will need to retrain their brain to think about risk in a new way to become a successful entrepreneur.

Creativity

Project and program managers are able to bring organization to chaos. But the reality is that creativity is often found in chaos. When you think about the stereotype of artists and other creative types, you probably don't think about their organizational skills. In fact, artists have a reputation for being unorganized. While this is not always true, there are reasons creative types have earned that reputation. If a project or program manager is going to do well as an entrepreneur, they need to look deep inside to ensure they have enough creativity to be effective. Creativity can also help program managers solve the problems that inevitably occur on complex programs. Fostering personal creativity can benefit you, no matter the role you are in.

Decisiveness

Project and program managers often gather information and present data so that stakeholders and sponsors can make decisions about a project or program. This is a very different skillset than actually making a decision. Leaders must make decisions based on incomplete data and own the consequences if the decision turns out to be a bad one. Before a project or program manager sets out to start a company, they should be sure they are comfortable making decisions.

Application to Project Management Professionals

Entrepreneurship is a popular focus area in MBA programs, so anyone considering an MBA should know whether they want to make it *their* area of focus. Many people dream of running their own company, and you may be one of them. I hope that this chapter helps you decide whether you would make a good entrepreneur, and whether getting an MBA can help you on that journey. But even if you stay in the project and program management profession, knowing more about entrepreneurship can help you in your career.

Unless you work for a government or nonprofit organization, there is going to be an entrepreneur who founded the company, so understanding the realities of starting and growing a company will help you to understand the decisions made by leadership. This especially applies if you are working for a new company. The founder may be seeking to take the organization public in the future, or maybe in the middle of seeking additional funding. Understanding these events can help you understand and motivate your teams to work toward these larger goals.

Additional Resources

Free textbook: https://open.umn.edu/opentextbooks/textbooks/entrepre-neurship-and-innovation-toolkit

Free textbook: https://open.umn.edu/opentextbooks/textbooks/law-for-entrepreneurs

Free textbook: https://open.umn.edu/opentextbooks/textbooks/sustain-ability-innovation-and-entrepreneurship

CHAPTER 8

Organizational Behavior and Human Resources

Why Study Organizational Behavior and Human Resources?

People are the engine for getting things done in any organization. Studying how people think and act so that you can get the best work out of people is an important management skill. It's even more important when you have responsibility without authority as project and program managers do.

Organizational behavior (OB) and human resources (HR) are different disciplines that both center on the people side of organizations. OB is sometimes considered a subset of HR, but it is a complex and important field with theories that have enormous application to project and program management as we work with, and through, other people. Traditional HR focuses a lot on the laws and mechanics of bringing people into and out of an organization. More modern HR organizations focus on training and enabling employees to thrive at work—but they do it by applying OB theory. OB is about understanding what motivates and enables employees to bring their best selves to work.

Mastering OB theory and HR principles will help project and program managers build high-functioning teams and navigate the many challenges that are encountered every day in projects. Do you need to build a better relationship with a difficult stakeholder? Are you having challenges with team members who are unmotivated? OB and HR can help you navigate these challenges. Project and program managers, by virtue of their leadership role in the organization, have the ability to influence team culture, both positively and negatively. The value of a positive team culture should not be underestimated.

Understanding the Basics

Managing Organizational Change

As the familiar quote from Heraclitus says: "The only constant in life is change."[1] Even though change happens all the time, many, if not most, people are resistant to change. There is an underlying fear of the unknown. This resistance to change is a substantial problem for organizations that must change continuously to stay ahead of market conditions. This puts a real tension between the organizational need to continuously change with the natural human condition of employees to resist change. Thus, an entire discipline has been built around managing organizational change.

Note that when we talk about organizational change, we are not necessarily talking about changes to roles and people in an organization—though it may include these kinds of changes too. We are talking about changing the way an organization operates, moves, thinks, or acts. Changing a company's core Enterprise Resource Planning (ERP) system will require organizational change management, as will a merger or acquisition, shutting down a division, and many other events.

When you think about project and program management in an organization, it is all about introducing change. Whether it is new technologies, processes, vendors, products, or services, projects deliver a new end state that an organization must adjust to, making the mastery of organizational change critical for project success.

In 2012, Harvard Professor John Kotter published a book titled *Leading Change*[2] that outlined eight steps for managing organizational change. This organizational change model was widely adopted, and in 2014, he updated those steps in his book *Accelerate*.[3] Any project or program manager who implements a project with impact to the way an organization works should become familiar with these processes. The eight steps of Kotter's model are outlined in the following sections.

Create a Sense of Urgency

To break through the general resistance to change, you will need to instill a sense of urgency for the change. External threats to the organization are a great way to stimulate a sense of urgency. The threat that a competitor may get a new product to market first can be very motivating. So can internal changes. New leadership with new ideas can drive a sense of urgency to change the status quo. Whatever you can tie your change to in order to create urgency will help you gain support around the need for change

Build a Guiding Coalition

When you need to make real organizational change, it is imperative to get support from all corners of the organization. This is more than passive buy-in. Creating a guiding coalition is about developing an active team of senior leaders who will help guide the change, then see that it gets pushed to the right levels of the organization. This coalition will need to be filled with respected leaders who have authority to act and enable change within the organization. Without this support, the risk of failure increases substantially.

Form a Strategic Vision and Initiatives

People must see the benefit of change to be motivated to start. If the changes negatively impact a person, then they at least need to understand the necessity before they will be accepting the change. They also need to have a vision for what the future will be like and their place in that new reality. The guiding coalition will need to pay close attention to drafting a vision that will allow the organization to rally behind it. People also need to believe that change can be achieved before they will rally behind it. To build credibility, leadership will need to show the steps, or initiatives, required to get to that vision.

Enlist a Volunteer Army

Once a vision is prepared, it is critical to share that vision with the rest of the organization. This is not a *one-and-done* activity. Sharing the vision and the resulting changes will need to repeated many times and in different ways for people to absorb the message. People learn in different ways, so preparing videos, conducting forums, sending e-mails, providing documentation, and other communication forms will ensure you are reaching all kinds of learners. Once the messaging *does* sink in, you are on your way to building a small army of advocates for the change.

Enable Action by Removing Obstacles

Obstacles to change take many forms. Obstacles can include lack of worker skills, lack of technology to support the change, lack of formal structures to support the change, and individual resistance (or refusal) to change. The guiding coalition must watch for these obstacles and actively counter them when they arise.

Generate Quick Wins

The value of quick wins should not be underestimated. Real, meaningful change is a long journey. It is easy to lose people along the way if they do not feel a sense of motion. To keep people excited about the change, you should plan for incremental wins. This is a similar concept to what drives the popularity of agile methodologies. Agile scrum teams demonstrate incremental progress on a regular basis, and that helps stakeholders see progress being made. Similarly, successful change campaigns will need to show quick wins to keep stakeholder interest.

Sustain Acceleration

As traction grows, it is important to go from strength to strength. Little wins should propel you to larger wins. This can be one of the longest phases of the change campaign. Once all the forums and e-mails stop, it is up to the guiding coalition to ensure that the seed that was planted grows to full size. This may require replacing managers or key employees that just haven't been able to navigate or support the change.

Institute Change

Once the change has grown sufficiently, it is up to leadership to embed this change into company culture and make it part of the organization's narrative and value structure.

By following Kotter's eight steps, we as project and program managers can develop and lead impactful changes that result from our projects. The better we are at managing the change we introduce into an organization, the more valuable we become to the organization. Implementing the change can be the easy part of the effort—gaining the ongoing support of people for the change can be the larger effort.

Organizational Structure and Power

The way an organization chooses to structure its reporting hierarchy can tell you a lot about it. Organizational structure is foundational to an organization, and many people do not give it much thought, but an organizational structure can help or hinder productivity. Organizational hierarchies are the formal power structure in an organization, but power and politics in an organization also live outside of the formal hierarchy.

To be an effective project and program manager, you need to read and understand how to navigate both formal and informal power structures in an organization. Formal hierarchies are easier to navigate because they are published by the organization to aid employees. Informal power structures are much more difficult to detect and navigate, but navigating them successfully could bear substantial fruit.

We will explore common organizational hierarchies, plus types of power outside of formal authority in subsequent sections.

Organizations tend to fall into two broad categories: centralized or decentralized. Traditional command and control structures exemplify the centralized hierarchy. Most large organizations of the past had well-defined, but centralized, decision-making pathways defined. Military organizations are highly centralized because centralized decision making is good when there is a lot of uncertainty, like when there is a crisis.

In recent years, organizations have explored more decentralized hierarchies. The idea is that those closest to the work will have the best information and, therefore, the best context to make decisions. This is a central idea behind the agile movement. Enabling scrum teams to self-manage is the epitome of a decentralized structure.

Table 8.1 shows the many heirarchies common in organizations.

Table 8.1 Common organizational hierarchies

Hierarchy type	Description
Functional	Functional organizations are built around specialized skillsets. They typically have separate teams for HR, IT, finance, product, sales, marketing, and so on. This is a very common type of organization. **Pros:** Pooling common skillsets creates economies of scale. **Cons:** Many layers of leadership between the top of the org and the lowest layers. Like the telephone game where messages get more confused with each connection, these structures can dilute top management, messaging to lower layers. Additionally, functional organizations are prone to creating silos between functions.
Flat	A flat organization attempts to cut out layers of hierarchy. Instead of a pyramid, it is more organic. **Pros:** The distance from the top to the bottom of the organization is short. Access to leadership is high. **Cons:** Decision making can be complex without a clearly defined structure. Also, flat organizations can have many employees reporting to a single manager, thus putting undue stress on the manager.
Product-based	Some organizations have learned that to get products to market faster and with better focus, they should organize based on those products. Each product team is headed by a general manager, and every facet of product design, development, production, sales, and support are handled within the product team. **Pros:** Strong product focus. **Cons:** Smaller teams can suffer from scale issues.
Matrix	Matrixed organizations combine functional and product-based structures. Most members of a matrix organization have dual reporting structures, one to the functional org, and a second to the product org (usually a dotted line without formal authority). This allows team members with similar talents (such as project and program managers) to be teamed together in a functional organization where they can be supported, but embedded with a product team where they can integrate with key product team members. **Pros:** Team members get the best of both worlds with a functional manager and product team to embed with. **Cons:** Complexity and potential conflicting priorities.

Other hierarchical structures exist as well but are largely variants of the preceding four hierarchies outlined, including some geographical and regions variations.

Types of Organizational Power

In 1959, a team of social psychologists, John French and Bertram Raven, published a work on the five bases of power.[4] Later, a sixth base was published. These bases of power have been generally accepted in industry and have been taught by business schools for years. Recognizing these types of power at work will help you navigate any organization with which you're affiliated.

Table 8.2 Types of organizational power

Power type	Description
Positional/ legitimate	Legitimate power is derived from hierarchical authority. A manager has legitimate authority to direct the work of subordinates. This positional authority may be legitimate, but it does not mean the subordinates will be inspired to do the work; they may do it solely out of duty. When a parent says to a child "do it because I said so," they are using their positional authority. Positional authority is the surest kind of authority, but it does not guarantee compliance for any reason other than fear of consequences.
Coercive	Coercive power uses fear to force others to do something they don't want to do. It can be physical, emotional, social, or other kinds of fear that motivate others to take action they don't want to take. The use of coercive power is not appropriate in a professional setting.
Reward	Reward power comes from the ability to give praise, recognition, promotion, money, or other kind of honor to another person. Often, it is a person's manager who can give these rewards, but not always. External awards and recognitions can drive and motivate people as successfully as internal reward potential. One easy way for a project and program manager to flex reward power is to recognize key team members in a public forum. By building a reputation as a project manager who publicly recognizes team members, you will earn a positive reputation.
Referent	Referent power is about relationships. It is about who a person knows. A person with a direct relationship with an organization founder may have outsized influence in the organization even if they have lower positional power. As you rise in the ranks of leadership, referent power becomes more important, and you are expected to bring a certain level of referent power to the role. You are expected to have relationships with other leaders in similar roles as a way to draw on outside ideas and best practices. Project and program managers have a unique opportunity to work with people across all corners of an organization. I have seen project managers with substantial referent power because of the projects they have worked on. They are able to connect across an organization in ways others cannot.

(Continued)

Table 8.2 (Continued)

Power type	Description
Expert	Expert power is when a person's knowledge is a source of power. The person(s) in an organization who created the product would hold expert power in addition to whatever positional power they may have. External recognitions, certifications, or degrees can also bolster a person's expert power. Project and program managers can gain expert power within their organizations by adding certifications, gaining degrees (such as an MBA), designing processes, and delivering difficult projects.
Informational	Informational power was added by Raven years after the original list of five was published. It may seem similar to expert power at first but has some important differences. As defined, informational power is the ability a person has to use logic to persuade those around them. The person does not need to have expert knowledge in the area to be persuasive. They are able to put information together in such a way it resonates with others. I have seen an alternate form of informational power in use around organizations. This is the information *hoarder*. Some people like to hold on to key information as a way to bolster their power in an organization. It is a bad thing for the organization and a temporary advantage for the individual. Be on the lookout for information hoarders in your organization. When you come upon them, find ways to carefully extract the information you need and publish it for others so that they can access it too.

Motivational Theory

Psychology and sociology are full of theories about how people work on the inside and how they interact with other humans. One area that has seen substantial research is related to motivating others. As you can imagine, this is an important subject for businesses, as they struggle to get employees to work with more urgency. There are so many theories that a full review of each would be a separate textbook on its own. For project and program managers, it is important to be aware of some of the more prominent theories in circulation. We will review three of these theories here, but I encourage you to access the additional resources at the end of the chapter to more thoroughly examine these, and other, motivational theories.

One thing to note—it is important that project and program managers know the boundaries between motivating employees and crossing the *people management line*. Some issues you may experience on your project teams are best handled by an employee's people manager, and maybe directly by HR. A rule of thumb is that if there is any chance the behavior could be considered misconduct, you should immediately involve the employee's direct manager.

Maslow's Hierarchy of Needs

One of the most referenced motivation theories was created by Abraham Maslow in 1943 in a paper titled *A Theory of Human Motivation*.[5] Within the paper, Maslow introduced his hierarchy of needs, which has become almost ubiquitous in its use in education and business settings. In my college education, I was taught this hierarchy no less than four times.

The reason it is ubiquitous is it's easy to understand and adaptable to many disciplines. The motivational theory he put forward was not actually grounded in much scientific research, but the concepts are so straightforward that they resonate with readers. It also has direct relevance for project and program managers.

The power of the theory is the assertion that people will not achieve the next level of the hierarchy until the needs of the current level are fulfilled. It also says that individuals do not like to be at the lower levels of the hierarchy for long and will strive to move up. Brief descriptions of each level in Maslow's hierarchy are as follows:

Level 1: Physiological needs—these are the basics to sustain human life such as food, water, and shelter. People will not be able to attend to other needs until they are comfortable their physiological needs are met.

Level 2: Safety needs—these are the need for stability, predictability, and order. Is their job stable, their neighborhood safe, and their future reasonably assured?

Level 3: Love and belongingness needs—these are about interpersonal relationships, intimacy, and acceptance from others.

Level 4: Esteem needs—these are about independence, dignity, and achievement.

Level 5: Self-actualization needs—these are about a person reaching their peak potential and achieving self-fulfillment.

When you have problems with project team members and stakeholders, it can be powerful to remember that they may not be able to focus on your project until they have satisfied whatever need they are struggling with at their present level. For example, you are not likely to get time from a key stakeholder to talk about a new project when they are busy putting out departmental fires. Their need to achieve stability (Level 2) is greater than their need to move the project work along (Level 4).

Herzberg's Two-Factor Theory

Like Maslow's theory, Fredrik Herzberg postulated that there are defined factors that need to be obtained for a person to feel satisfied. In the 1960s, Herzberg put forward this theory in his article *One More Time: How Do You Motivate Employees,*[6] but added a new dimension by asserting that there is a second set of defined factors that determine dissatisfaction in a person. According to the theory, this second list of dissatisfaction factors is independent from the list of satisfaction factors, meaning that a person can feel both high satisfaction and dissatisfaction at the same time.

Some of Herzberg's factors contributing to satisfaction include achievement, recognition, growth, and responsibility. Some of the factors contributing to dissatisfaction are: work conditions, status, supervisor, and company policies.

Herzberg's theory has some interesting impacts for project and program managers. At a personal level, it is instructive to think about the ways our job both satisfies and dissatisfies us. For example, two of the satisfaction dimensions are achievement and recognition. As project and program managers, we need to find a situation where we can feel achievement and gain recognition. It is also important that we help our team members feel the same. But even these factors may not offset other factors on the dissatisfaction scale such as our relationship with our manager, our peers, or our compensation.

The bottom line is that a person may leave an organization even when feeling substantial satisfaction in some areas if the levels of dissatisfaction in other areas are high enough. Guarding ourselves and our team members against dissatisfaction will help keep good talent in the organization, and we will be happier as a result.

Expectancy Theory

Expectancy theory was first postulated by Yale professor Victor H. Vroom in 1964.[7] This theory is also focused on employee motivation and says that people will change their behavior based on expected reward. For example, an employee will work more hours at night if there is a reasonable expectation that behavior will bring a reward like promotion or a raise.

The theory is built on three primary factors: expectancy, instrumentality, and valence.

1. Expectancy is the belief that you will be able to meet the performance expectation.
2. Instrumentality is the belief that you will actually get the reward if you meet the expectation.
3. Valence is the value you place on the expected reward. These factors interplay with each other and determine the level of motivation a person has related to the effort.

Conflict Resolution

Conflict in the workplace is inevitable. Many business professionals, professors of business, and workplace researchers go so far as to say conflict in the workplace is healthy because it means multiple perspectives are being considered and the best ideas are likely to survive. It's easy to see why conflict in the workplace exists. All organizations exist in a state of scarcity (remember our economics lessons in Chapter 2!). Scarcity of time, budget, people, and other resources create an environment where trade-offs must continuously be evaluated. It is often these points of trade-off where conflict arises. Thus, given the reality of conflict in the workplace, it is important to learn strategies to effectively manage and work through these conflicts.

Project and program managers are specially placed to see and experience conflicts due to the nature of our work. As a profession, we are pushing boundaries and creating new realities within an organization, and this sets us up to be at a conflict focal point. What, then, can we do to manage conflict?

Conflict theories include many options for resolution, but some of those options are not appropriate in the workplace, such as use of violence. We will discuss three common and work-appropriate approaches in the next section.

Avoid the Conflict

Conflict avoidance may be one of the most common responses. Most, but not all, people would prefer to avoid conflict than have to deal with it directly. Those avoiding conflict hope the problem will go away in time. The problem is, hope is not a strategy. Some conflicts *will* go away, but many will get worse over time. Unless there are valid reasons to believe the conflict will go away, avoidance is not a recommended strategy, especially for a project manager. Conflicts are risks to successfully completing a project and should be dealt with professionally and promptly.

Accommodate the Conflict

When one accommodates the conflict, they give in to the other party's side of the argument. Accommodation is both better and worse than avoidance because it at least faces the conflict, but it caves in without any further engagement. If we buy into the idea conflict is healthy, then this strategy does not allow for the positive effects of conflict to be realized. Project managers should not just accommodate conflicts unless the accommodation of the conflict somehow helps the success of the project.

Lean Into the Conflict

This is the only option that helps an organization sort through its options in an effective way. Confrontation does not mean to react aggressively but to act with intention when conflict arises. There are several proven techniques to assist as you lean into the conflict.

Accept That Conflict Is Normal

This is about changing our own attitudes toward conflict. While most people dislike conflict, coming to realize at both an intellectual and emotional level that conflict is normal can help us to reshape our response when it inevitably arises. This is also a good starting point when trying to find common ground.

Find Common Ground

This is about helping all parties to recognize that a conflict exists, that it is healthy, and that there are areas on which all sides can agree. Starting with common ground is a great way to reduce emotion and encourage all sides that a resolution can be found.

Brainstorm Solutions

Once common ground is found, jointly discuss options that could accommodate the most important concerns of each party. Keep proper perspective that you will likely have to bend on points that are important to you, but so should the other party.

Determine the Next Steps

If the brainstorming session(s) goes well, the next steps may be easy because the conflict is resolved. If it did not yield a result, you must determine if you will continue discussions or not. If not, you will need to resolve what happens when neither party is satisfied. Perhaps, it is an escalation to senior management, or similar alternative. If continued discussion is desired, be clear on the next steps and ensure they are followed until both parties are satisfied.

Negotiation

Negotiation is commonly considered a specialized form of conflict resolution and is grounded in similar theory because both are about reconciling two separate perspectives. Many people would prefer to negotiate than to be involved in a conflict, but negotiation can still cause stress. One of the key differences is that in most cases, people voluntarily enter into a negotiation. When purchasing a car, taking a new job, buying a home, or brokering some other deal, these are situations that are typically entered into by choice.

Popular literature on negotiation is filled with tips and tricks for gaining an edge in negotiations. Even Donald Trump published a book on it in 1987 titled *Art of the Deal*,[8] which gives his perspective on negotiation. These books tend to be written by practitioners of negotiation (business people, hostage negotiators, etc.) rather than academic studies specific to negotiation. However, there are a few academic approaches to negotiating, which are outlined as follows.

Principled Negotiation

The *Harvard Negotiation Project*[9] has existed since 1979 and produced the concept of *principled negotiation*. This concept was summarized in *Getting to Yes* by Roger Fisher and William Ury.[10] This book has been a staple of business literature for nearly three decades. It attempts to strip out the emotional aspects of negotiation by focusing on the problem not the people. It focuses on interests, not positions.

Game Theory

While typically considered an economic theory, game theory has been adapted and advanced in multiple disciplines, including conflict resolution and negotiation. Game theory allows people engaged in a negotiation or conflict (players) to develop a set of actions to take (strategy) for the negotiation (game) based on likely interactions. A key assumption is that players will act rationally and seek the best outcome for themselves (payout). As the game unfolds, individual actions impact the outcome.

To better understand the interplay involved in game theory, let's look at a classic game theory example called the prisoner's dilemma.

Prisoner's Dilemma

Imagine two criminals (players) commit a crime and get arrested for it. The police have no hard evidence so must get a confession to move forward with the conviction. The police move each criminal into a separate room to attempt to get confessions (game).

To understand the dynamics faced by each criminal, we must understand the potential consequences for each possible outcome (payout). If the criminals cooperate with each other by not confessing, both walk free.

If both confess, both get five years in prison. If one cuts a deal with the police and confesses, and one does not, then the one who confesses gets a deal of only two years in prison, and the other gets a severe sentence of 10 years. Figure 8.1 shows the possible outcomes visually.

The best possible option for the criminals is for both to stay silent, but because they are separated, they cannot tell what their partner is going to do. The worst outcome is for their partner to flip on them while they stay silent because they will get the maximum sentence. If they confess, their outcome is either two years or five years, both better outcomes than the maximum punishment.

Game theory tells us that each criminal, as rational actors, will understand the stakes. If there is substantial trust between the criminals, they may be willing to risk not talking—but in most cases, they will understand that confessing is the safest, most rational way to proceed (strategy).

When we apply game theory to negotiations, we can play out the possible scenarios and payoffs, and thus, when in the negotiation, we can know what moves to make at each step. While this kind of preparation for a negotiation can be substantial, there are times where the principles of game theory can be very valuable in preparing for and managing negotiations.

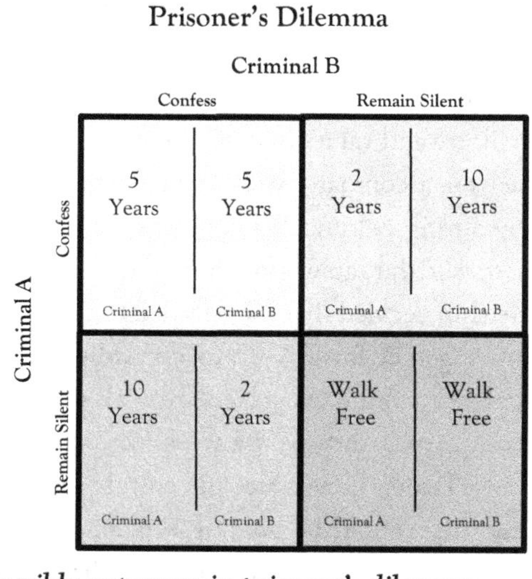

Prisoner's Dilemma

Figure 8.1 Possible outcomes in prisoner's dilemma

Building Culture

One of the more important focus areas of leadership is developing a strong and vibrant organization culture. In Chapter 1, we learned about the importance of a company's vision and mission in establishing corporate strategy. However, vision and mission are also critical to building a strong organizational culture, and a strong organizational culture provides managers and employees guardrails for how to behave and handle key situations.

The benefits of building a strong culture primarily accrue on the people side of the organization. For example, a strong culture can be a key part of an organization's retention strategy. A strong culture helps employees build a shared identity. New employees are introduced to the organization culture, and they start to adopt the shared culture as their own. This helps with retention and can also be used as a marketing device for recruiters to attract talent to the organization.

Building a strong organizational culture starts with careful examination of vision, mission, and values. If these don't exist yet (when an organization is new), then using the founder(s) vision and values can serve as a starting place. Once leadership knows what kind of culture they want to build, they will need to do frequent communication about the ideal culture and provide real-world examples of the organization's culture in action. Leaders must be the champions of company culture and actively work to preserve it. Each new employee who joins an organization can dilute the culture if there is not an active program to teach and foster the adoption of the culture and values in each employee.

I once worked for a company with a very strong set of values and a correspondingly strong culture. While I was there, senior leadership became concerned that the rapid growth of the company was diluting the culture. Leadership decided that they needed to bring all people managers into a room together for a week to do additional reinforcement of company values and culture. Managers from all corners of the world were flown to headquarters and spent a week learning directly from the founders and C-level leaders how values and culture shaped the company early on and how they should be guiding the company in the future. The hard costs to hold this meeting were likely in the millions of dollars, not including productivity loss. But senior leadership felt the investment would pay dividends in years to come. The very fact the company went to that length to preserve its culture spoke volumes about its commitment to culture and also demonstrated the value of culture in the organization.

Ethics

Some people that are cynical about corporations might say corporate ethics is an oxymoron, but the reality is ethics in business are frequently discussed and are often part of regular corporate training programs. The study of ethics is a vast field filled with books and treatises from philosophers and ethicists—some dating back millennia. Business ethics focus specifically on employee and management behavior and interactions. This includes activities such as handling of financial matters, treatment of other employees, and anything a person in an organization could potentially use to get unlawful gain. The definition of business ethics, according to the Cambridge dictionary is *the study of rules, principles, and beliefs about what is morally right or wrong when doing business.*[11]

There are several ethical approaches that can help a person or organization navigate ethical issues. When faced with an ethical situation in the workplace, it can be helpful to run the situation through the major ethical lenses outlined as follows.

Consequentialism

This approach is focused on the *outcomes,* or consequences, of an action. One of the biggest consequentialist frameworks is utilitarianism. This framework tells us that we should take the action that has the best outcome for the most people (or the least harm to the most people). It recognizes that some harm is certain to come from the decision, but that the decision taken should minimize the harm.

Non-Consequentialism

This approach dismisses the focus on outcomes and says that the *intention* of the action is the most important factor. One framework under this approach, deontology, focuses on ethical behavior as a duty that must be performed. First put forth by Immanuel Kant in the 18th century, deontology focuses on *categorical imperatives*, which are broad maxims for living, such as "always speak truthfully."

Agent-Centered

This approach is characterized by the idea that our actions should conform to ideal human behavior. One of the most recognized frameworks within this approach is virtue ethics, which was proposed by Aristotle in the 4th century BC and emphasizes that a person should strive to live an ethical life, not just use ethics for specific situations.

Application to Project and Program Managers

This chapter focused on the people side of an MBA education. As stated at the beginning of this chapter, mastering tools and techniques for optimizing interactions with people will provide enormous dividends for project and program managers. Our ability to influence without authority requires us understand and navigate delicate, complex interactions with team members, stakeholders, and others for the success of our projects.

While other chapters in this book will give you new tools for advancing technical aspects of your project management skillset, this chapter (and the next) gives you ideas to improve what might be the most critical aspect of our profession: working with people to accomplish important work of the organization. I recommend you refer to this chapter frequently and expand your studies of the concepts introduced here.

Additional Resources

Free OB textbook: https://open.umn.edu/opentextbooks/textbooks/30

Free business ethics textbook: https://open.umn.edu/opentextbooks/textbooks/617

Overview of change management process: https://kotterinc.com/8-steps-process-for-leading-change/

Free game theory textbook: http://faculty.econ.ucdavis.edu/faculty/bonanno/PDF/GT_book.pdf

Kotter website for change: https://www.kotterinc.com/8-steps-process-for-leading-change/

CHAPTER 9

Leadership

Why Study Leadership?

Where human resources (HR) and organizational behavior (OB) focus on helping employees perform at their best, the study of leadership is focused on improving the skills of individual leaders in order to maximize their effectiveness. The idea of what makes a person a leader is almost continuously debated. Television and other media deluge us with their stereotypes of how leaders are supposed to act. We see elected politicians who are both hailed as world leaders and derided as incompetent for the same actions. It is commonly agreed, though, that the primary role of leaders is to get results.

Understanding leadership is important to project and program managers because we lead the efforts of other people. It's also important to understand the difference between leaders and managers. We have the word *manager* in our titles, but we don't usually have positional authority for employees. In this chapter, we will explore the key concepts of leadership in an effort to advance our ability to be effective within an organization.

Understanding the Basics

Manager Versus Leader

The terms manager and leader are often used interchangeably in a casual conversation. The term *leader* is often preferred as it generally holds more cachet, but are managers and leaders really interchangeable? We'll look at what business literature says about the subject in subsesequent sections.

Most business literature draws a clear distinction between the skills of a manager and those of a leader. Managers focus on operations and execution. Good managers bring order to chaos and seek to achieve results for the organization. Leaders, on the other hand, set vision, ignite passion, and inspire the organization to think and act differently. They are change agents. It is said that employees work for managers but follow leaders. The good news is one is not necessarily more important than the other, and organizations need both skillsets to thrive.

Since we have now established these are different skillsets, then it's important to understand the answers to a few questions.

Can Leadership and Management Be Learned?

The good news for those who have never been managers or leaders is that most scholars believe management and leadership skills can be learned. Some people seem to be born with more natural leadership or management abilities than others, so the trajectory and altitude of how far one can build their skills may have some limits—but most people can build on their inborn talents to strengthen their abilities.[1]

Can a Person Be Both a Manager and Leader?

The answer is yes; people can be both strong managers and strong leaders. However, there is some debate as to whether *all* people can be both. The characteristics of each discipline are different enough that many consider it a rare thing for a person to be both good manager and good leader. Still, others insist that managers have to have some leadership abilities to be effective, and vice versa. While we will not settle the debate here, we will focus on the fact that each of us has some natural abilities that we can unlock with practice.

Is It Better for a Project Manager to Be a Leader or a Manager?

The answer to this may be in the question. The fact that our title contains *manager* is a good hint as to what skillset may be more valuable. Being the steady, planning, consistent manager is often the right set of characteristics to bring to project work. I hope this is not disappointing; I know that people want to be *leaders*. I think being a manager is essential to business success and is not to be trivialized. An organization needs more managers than leaders, or it could become paralyzed with competing visions and not enough skills to implement any of them.

While I believe management skills are, on balance, more important for project and program managers, there is definitely a place for leadership in our profession. Inspiring team members to rally behind the goals of the project, persuading stakeholders to make the right decision, helping people to push beyond their limitations, these are all leadership skills that project managers should add to their professional toolkits. These skills can help a person grow from a good project manager to a great one.

Project and program managers who employ leadership skills while running programs are able to create and maintain alignment among the team as changes and complexities surface. Thus, leadership skills are an important value-add to our role, raising the bar on what we are able to deliver.

Leadership Archetypes

A study of leadership has to start with a look at the types of leaders that exist in the world. To say that a leader falls into only one category is overly simplistic, but most leaders have a primary leadership style, with one or more secondary styles that they can use to drive results. No leader, though, is master of all leadership styles. The primary archetypes are as follows:

Transformational

The hallmark of the transformational style of leadership is that it inspires and motivates others to work hard to achieve organization goals. This is the kind of leader that takes to a stage and passionately paints a vision for what is possible. Transformational leaders inspire followers to take on large and difficult tasks by helping them feel like they can actually do it.

Transformational leaders sometimes appeal to moral aspects to inspire others. They set an example that others try to emulate. They help others express their creativity and push people to think in new and different ways. People follow transformational leaders because they become inspired by the vision. It can be more about the vision than the leader.

Charismatic

Charismatic leaders use their personality and charm to persuade followers to adopt their cause. Charismatic leaders, like transformational leaders, are able to passionately explain their vision to their followers, but charismatic leaders tend to focus on their own vision for the future, rather than on a shared vision of how things could be. People follow charismatic leaders because of who they are, then secondarily what they espouse.

The movements started by charismatic leaders sometimes struggle to continue without the leader at the head. If a charismatic leader moves on, organizations can struggle to continue implementing thier vision.

Ethical

Ethical leadership focuses on honesty, integrity, trust, and fairness. Ethical leaders display these characteristics at work, but they also display these traits outside of work. Ethical leaders behave the same way even when their behavior cannot be observed. Consistency in behavior is a major hallmark of this leadership style.

To some, the ethical style of leadership can appear weak, but ethical leaders are known to be able to make difficult decisions, especially when they are dealing with unethical behavior within the workplace. Leaders who embrace the ethical style of leadership seek to create an organization that also embraces ethical principles. It is believed that ethically oriented organizations have lower employee turnover and other benefits.

Laissez-faire

Laissez-faire is a French phrase that translates into English as *let you do*. It exemplifies a hands-off attitude to management and governance. The underlying belief of laissez-faire leadership is to hire talented people, then get out of their way to let them deliver. There are not governance structures or leadership direction that will add to the performance of those talented employees. It is the opposite of the autocratic leadership archetype.

Due to the hands-off nature of this leadership style, it is not appropriate for all industries and all types of employees. It works best for organizations with strong entrepreneurial values and with a high percentage of professionals (such as architects, engineers, lawyers, etc.). These employees are able to organize themselves and their work. They execute at a high professional level. Laissez-faire leadership does not work with employees who are in early stages of their career or who need a lot of direction to be effective. It is also not a good leadership style when an organization is experiencing a crisis that requires strong, centralized leadership. Critics of Laissez-faire leadership argue that the hands-off approach can allow a harmful culture to develop if leaders do not act ethically, because they are not closely monitored.

Bureaucratic

Bureaucratic leaders create a series of policies, procedures, hierarchies, and leadership chains to carefully manage the work being done. Bureaucratic leaders believe in structure and consistency through implementation of process. Government agencies are the stereotypical bureaucratic organizations and the people who lead them are often referred to as bureaucrats. We have all experienced situations where paperwork and process take the place of common sense. But are bureaucrats and bureaucracies bad?

Bureaucratic practices can benefit industries that operate under strict oversight such as financial markets, medical device manufacturing, and drug manufacturing. When strict, traceable consistency is required, bureaucratic leadership can help organizations navigate the challenges of highly regulated industries. The downside to bureaucratic leadership is that innovation can be stifled by all of the process in place. It is also hard to inspire hard work from employees when they feel like they are mired in process.

Autocratic

Similar to the bureaucratic leadership style, autocratic leadership focuses on process and consistent outcomes, but it differs in that autocrats focus power on the person, not the process. In autocratic organizations, all important decisions are made by the leader, and it is expected that all employees will strictly carryout those decisions.

While autocratic leadership has fallen out of favor in business, it remains a remarkably common leadership style. Autocratic leadership style is very common in military organizations, but is also surprisingly common in top-performing athletic organizations. Several famous coaches are notorious autocrats, but the results they are able to deliver show the inherent strength of this type of leadership.

Criticism of this archetype centers on the fact that most of the world's worst actors in history were all autocratic. Dictators and tyrants have used this style to suppress opposition and retain strict authority. It is also the first leadership style that some inexperienced leaders run to as they learn to navigate challenges.

Is There a Style of Leadership That Is Better Suited for Project and Program Managers?

This question is answered most easily by first eliminating the types of leadership that are inappropriate for project and program managers. The leadership style that is least compatible with our profession is laissez-faire due to its lack of oversight and governance. While ethical leadership can yield positive organizational results, there are not many specific aspects of that archetype that will help project managers lead the work.

The leadership types that lend themselves best to project management are transformational, charismatic, bureaucratic, and autocratic. These leadership styles either allow for inspiring team members to achieve their best or create environments where process and authority directly enable completion of goals.

The real question is whether people can change their leadership style to adapt to changing circumstances. In the next section, we will explore the fluidity of leadership.

Developing Leadership Styles

There is strong evidence that people can change and adapt their leadership styles to match a given situation. One theory, the Hersey and Blanchard situational leadership model,[2] is based on the idea that leaders not only can, but should, change their style. Hersey and Blanchard put forward that leaders change their style based on the maturity of and relationship with employees and co-workers. They assert that no leadership style is better than another, and each has its place in a modern organization. Instead of the six leadership archetypes outlined earlier, they define four styles:

1. *Delegating Style*—similar to the laissez-faire archetype, this style gives extensive autonomy to employees and is best when employees are highly skilled and mature.
2. *Participating Style*—this is a highly interactive style and is very supportive of employees. These leaders use praise and feedback to bolster employees. However, this style does not do much directing on basic tasks, preferring to trust that employees will rise to the challenge.
3. *Selling Style*—this is a high coaching and high task-focus style that is best in organizations where employees are motivated but not highly skilled.
4. *Telling Style*—similar to the autocratic archetype, this style is low on relationship and high on task focus. It is best suited to organizations where there is low employee maturity and skills.

The degree to which leaders can actually move between these four styles is debated. It is thought that leaders tend to have a dominant or natural style that they prefer to use, but that they can, with work, learn the other styles, though it may not feel natural to them.

Leadership Aptitude and Testing

How do you find out what kind of a leader you are? You may instinctively know you tend toward one style more than another. If you want external confirmation there are literally dozens of personality and leadership assessments that can help you determine your leadership style. While in my final year at Haas, the entire class participated in an offsite retreat in a beautiful California seaside location. Part of that offsite included receiving the results of a leadership assessment we'd completed earlier. The assessment used was the *Belbin Individual Report*,[3] which assessed our natural roles in a team setting. As each of us read through our assessments, it was remarkable to watch and listen to people react to the results. Some people felt it was as though the assessment read their minds and thoughts. The report did not mince words, though, and there were observations that allowed each of us to reflect on the insights and, potentially, improve our leadership ability.

Several reputable tests, including the Belbin test, are introduced next. If you have not yet taken a self-assessment test, there is a way that may help you determine your leadership style. Ask yourself what kind of leader you have liked and followed in the past. Think about those characteristics that resonated with you, and you may see that you had an affinity for that leader because they display qualities that you not only admire, but that are similar to your own natural abilities. While this may not be as accurate as one of the following self-assessment tools, it is an interesting thought exercise.

DISC Assessment

The DISC assessment[4] is one of the most common personality tests in use today. DISC is an acronym for the four dimensions measured by the tool. They are:

Dominance

This dimension measures the person's focus on getting things done. It is about confidence and the emphasis a person places on winning. People who have high scores in this dimension are more direct in the way they speak and can be criticized for being too blunt and lacking empathy for others.

Influence

This dimension is about persuasion, optimism, connection, and collaboration. People with high scores along this dimension thrive on interactions with others and get frustrated when their opinions and input are not taken seriously. In some ways, they are opposite from those high on dominance because they are sometimes criticized for not getting to the point quickly enough and not being focused.

Steadiness

This dimension is about calm, measured cooperation. People who score high on this dimension are known for being dependable, expressing appreciation, and acting carefully. They do not like to be rushed, and approval of those around them is important. They can be criticized for being too slow, not changing direction quickly enough, and they tend to avoid confrontation. Working with people high in this dimension can be hard for those high on the dominance scale.

Conscientiousness

This dimension is about attention to detail, accuracy, and expertise. People who score high on this dimension are often in professions where details matter, such as engineering or medicine. They gain personal satisfaction from producing high-quality work results. They are rational thinkers and like to grow their professional skillsets. People who are high on this dimension are criticized for being rigid and unable to delegate because of concerns about quality. It can also take them a long time to make a decision because they need to be sure of the outcome.

Part of the reason the DISC assessment is popular is because it can be done online, and results are immediately available. While the results can be understood by those who take the test, there can be benefit to having the results reviewed by experts trained in the DISC assessment to help interpret the results and highlight areas where a person could be in a mismatched role.

There are multiple providers of DISC assessments, with some being more reputable than others. If you want to take the DISC assessment for yourself, look for trusted names who administer the exam.

Is There a Preferred DISC Type for Project Managers?

If you look at the DISC dimensions, it is easy to see that each one has strengths and drawbacks for project and program managers. Dominance is important because there must be enough confidence and focus to really drive the work of the project. However, their bluntness and struggles with empathy could make it hard for them to develop healthy team dynamics. The same plus and minus dynamic goes with influencing and the other dimensions. If you take the DISC assessment, the recommendation is to carefully examine your strongest dimensions and leverage your strengths while remaining aware of the inherent weaknesses. The benefit of these types of assessments is they allow you to personally reflect on ways to improve yourself.

Enneagram of Personality

One of the more controversial personality assessments, the Enneagram of Personality, has seen a recent resurgence in business and across the Internet. The history of Enneagram is a little murky, and some psychologists take issue with the science behind it,[5] but the momentum of this assessment in the marketplace is undeniable.

The Enneagram of Personality defines nine personality types plotted on a circle, with interconnection shown between types. According to the assessment, everyone has a primary personality type that forms in childhood, but that individuals have natural affinity to other personality types, called wings. Additionally, the nine types are grouped into three centers that further show common characteristics. The three centers are instinctive, feeling, and thinking.

The nine primary personality types of the Enneagram of Personality are shown in Table 9.1.

Table 9.1 Enneagram of Personality—nine personality types

Type	Name	Major attributes
1	Reformer	Rational, idealistic, self-controlled
2	Helper	Caring, generous, people-oriented, sacrificing
3	Achiever	Driven by success, seeks excellence, concerned with image
4	Individualist	Sensitive, withdrawn but expressive, self-conscious, temperamental
5	Investigator	Intense, perceptive, alert, secretive, withdrawn
6	Loyalist	Reliable, committed, engaging, anxious, fear-driven
7	Enthusiast	Spontaneous, optimistic, energetic, scattered
8	Challenger	Decisive, strong-willed, confrontational
9	Peacemaker	Good-natured, accepting, complacent, resigned

Myers–Briggs-Type Indicator (MBTI)[6]

Arguably one of the oldest personality assessments, it is still used by many organizations today. The psychological underpinnings of the Myers–Briggs-type indicator (MBTI) are based on the work by noted psychoanalyst Carl Jung. The outcome of the MBTI is a reading on your personality type. The type is based on four dimensions, each with two possible outcomes.

- *Extroversion (E) or Introversion (I):* This is your preference for where you focus. Do you like to live in the outside world, or in your personal inner world? The *E* or *I* is the first letter in the four-letter MBTI.
- *Sensing (S) or Intuition (N):* This is how you intake information. Those who use sensing look at reality and facts. They look for practical use of the information. Those using intuition will interpret the data to see possibilities. They enjoy exploring ideas and concepts, and can sometimes be poetic.
- *Thinking (T) or Feeling (F):* This is your preferred way of making decisions. Those that prefer thinking like to rely on facts and data. They make decisions impersonally and look for logical flaws in arguments. Those who use feeling to make decisions tend to think outside themselves. They are sometimes described as empathetic and look at the impact of the decision on personal values and ramification on others.
- *Judging (J) or Perceiving (P):* This is how you deal with the outside world. Judging types like to have clear instructions and make careful plans before stepping out the door. Those who are on the perceiving end of the spectrum prefer to keep options open, to improvise based on changing information, and be spontaneous.

The result of the MBTI will be an assessment of your personality type in a series of four letters corresponding to the preceding type indicators, along with descriptions of your primary tendencies.

Is There an MBTI That Is Better for Project Managers?

A study was done at the Graziadio Business School at Pepperdine University[7] that yielded some interesting insights into the most common Meyers–Briggs indicators of project managers participating in the study. The study looked at the MBTI scores of 202 project managers and identified the most common traits across each of the four trait areas. Interestingly, the most common type was ISTJ, or introspective, sensing, thinking, and judging. This personality type is described this way by the Myers–Briggs Foundation:

> Quiet, serious, earn success by thoroughness and dependability. Practical, matter-of-fact, realistic, and responsible. Decide logically what should be done and work toward it steadily, regardless of distractions. Take pleasure in making everything orderly and organized—their work, their home, their life. Value traditions and loyalty.[8]

If this sounds like you—take heart! You're in good company. There is no indication in the study that this personality type is more successful than other personality types at running projects, just the frequency of trait type. It is likely that the variety of project and organization types will allow for a large variety of successful project management personality types.

John Maxwell Leadership Assessment

Based on John Maxwell's book *Five Levels of Leadership*,[9] this assessment looks at a person's ability to lead and influence based on his five levels of leadership:

1. *Position:* People follow this level of leadership because they have to.
2. *Permission:* People follow this level of leadership because they want to.
3. *Production:* People follow this level of leadership because of your contributions to the organization.
4. *People Development:* People follow this level of leadership because of what you personally did to help them in their career.
5. *Pinnacle:* People follow you because of who you are.

This instrument uses a 360-degree perspective, meaning it assesses an individual based on feedback from those who report to you, those who are colleagues to you, and those who are above you in the management chain. Unlike the DISC and Meyers–Briggs, this assessment is focused directly on leadership ability, not just on personality traits and behaviors.

Belbin Assessments

Belbin has four different assessments for individuals and teams. These assessments are not especially well known, but I include them because the assessment for individuals was used during my MBA program, and I found it personally enlightening. The assessments are based on the work of Dr. Meredith Belbin, a British psychologist who focused his studies on work-related interactions.

Dr. Belbin defined nine roles that naturally develop in a team, called Belbin Team Roles.[10] The team-based assessments are used to show the roles (not titles) people are filling in a team and help team members achieve better balance in a team, so it can perform better. Each report shares insights about the participant's strengths and weaknesses.

A case can be made that for critical, high-impact projects, developing a high-performing team will be critical. An assessment tool that looks at team dynamics and gives suggestions for performance improvements could be of great value.

Leading Without Authority

When a formal reporting structure exists between manager and employee, there are tools the manager can use to provide incentives for getting good work from employees, as well as reprimands for poor work performance. Raises, bonuses, and the reductions of the same give managers leverage to coax performance from employees. What happens when you don't have that same leverage, but still need performance from individuals? This is the challenge of every project and program manager. The good news is there are still many levers you can pull to get good performance from employees.

Some may try to argue that it is not the role of the project and program manager to change the behavior of a team member, but a good project and program manager will always strive to resolve issues and help those around them reach their best possible performance levels. When a project and program manager seeks to improve those around them, they not only help their project, they help themselves. Project managers will earn a reputation among team members such that team members will ask to be assigned to their projects. This kind of positive reputation will make future projects easier to manage because they will have a motivated team.

The opposite is also true. A project manager who treats team members poorly, betrays trust, or drives team members without empathy will earn a negative reputation that will hinder work in future projects. Once a project manager has lost the ability to get good performance from team members, they are of little use to the organization.

Improving on Already Good Performance

If you are fortunate enough to be managing a project where team members are generally working well, you should count yourself lucky. You should not take it for granted. You should look for ways to turn a team that is performing reasonably well into a high-performing team. The key to increasing the performance of a team is to understand what motivates the individual team members, then find a common vision for the team to rally behind. In the prior chapter, we learned about what motivates an individual. We will apply those learnings to provide you ideas for improving performance, without having actual authority over team members.

The first thing to recognize is that each individual will be motivated by a cluster of actions that will be unique to them. As you work closely with each individual, you will want to take note of how they respond to different situations and different motivations. Some will enjoy public recognition, others private notes of appreciation. Some will respond to challenges, others to an empathetic ear. If you have problems detecting what will motivate individuals on your team, it is completely appropriate to ask individuals what they respond to and what motivates them. People enjoy talking about themselves, so don't be afraid to be direct.

Motivation is complex, but Table 9.2 lists many techniques for motivating individuals to perform their best.

Table 9.2 Motivational techniques

Motivational tool	Best for	Ideas for implementation
Public recognition	• Those who seek external validation • Those seeking positive feedback for promotion or advancement	Most organizations will have employee recognition mechanisms you can use. If not, raise the idea to leadership.
Private recognition	• Those who value personal relationships	Send an e-mail or direct message to the employee. Recognize their work in a 1:1 meeting.
Notes to management	• Those seeking positive feedback for promotion or advancement	Use messages to stakeholders as an opportunity to call out high performers. Send direct messages to the employee's manager praising the work.
Challenges and variety	• Those who are high on the dominance scale in the DISC assessment • Those eager to show off their skills	Assign high-profile projects to high performers. Give special assignments to these employees.
Group pressure	• Those who don't like to follow process	Develop positive recognition mechanisms for those who follow processes that are shared publicly. Also, use public e-mails/statuses to highlight those who have completed assignments and those who have not. It's a more neutral way to publicly bring attention to those who haven't completed their work. It also leaves things neutral in case they have completed, but it somehow fell through the cracks.

Application to Project and Program Management

Whether you consider yourself a manager or a leader (or both!), the tools discussed in this chapter (as well as the previous) are a valuable way to improve your skills. Recent thinking on leadership shows that it can be a fluid concept, and that while most people have a dominant style, many people are able to flexibly apply leadership concepts from different styles. Knowing when to apply the various styles to a situation takes experience but is a worthwhile journey. It will not only help your organization, but your professional career as well.

Many assessments exist to help you understand your personal attributes and leadership tendencies. These are a good way to take an honest look at your strengths as well as your opportunity areas. I encourage you to take advantage of these opportunities as they come up in your career. If you have not yet had the opportunity to take an assessment, I recommend finding a reputable one that is inexpensive, and take it online. You will certainly learn a lot about yourself.

Additional Resources

A Forbes, Inc. list of the best leadership books: https://www.forbes.com/sites/micahsolomon/2019/06/22/best-leadership-books/?sh=7a7c0e4f1fa0

DISC assessments: https://www.discprofile.com/what-is-disc

Myers–Briggs assessment: https://www.myersbriggs.org/

Belbin assessment: https://belbinnorthamerica.com/a-guide-to-belbin-team-roles/

CHAPTER 10

Is an MBA Right for You?

If you've ever thought about getting an MBA, this chapter is for you. I believe getting an MBA is valuable, but not for all people, and not in all ways they are delivered. There are many considerations to take into account when making a decision as big as this. An MBA will stretch you personally and professionally. It will vacuum up all available time you have. It may cause you to take on student loan debt. Whether the benefits of the MBA are greater than the cost you pay (in time, effort, and money) is not guaranteed, either—so you must give it careful consideration.

In this chapter, we will explore key questions: Should you do a full-time MBA, or one designed for working professionals? Do you go for the best college you can get into, or a local (or online) program? Should you do it now, or in the future? Will it give you the benefit you're hoping for? We will consider how each of these play into your decision.

What Is It Really Like?

Prior to my MBA, I earned a bachelor's degree (BA) in Communications from Brigham Young University, and a Master of Science (MS) in Student Affairs from Florida State University. I was well acquainted with college life, admissions tests, and the like. But the MBA was different from either of my previous experiences.

Even getting into business school was more rigorous than the other programs I'd been in. I easily spent a year in preparation for the application process. This includes time spent studying for, and taking the GMAT, as well as taking MBA pre-requisite classes required by the schools I applied to (accounting, statistics, and calculus). You may have a head start if you have a more business or mathematical background than I did.

The application process can be pretty tedious too. You will likely need transcripts from any schools you attended. You will need to write essays and, in some cases, pass interviews. Not all schools require this level of rigor, but the better ones do. In addition to all that work, you also get to send in an application fee, which may not sound like much, but when you apply to multiple schools, it can start to add up.

I applied to four different schools. UC Berkeley's Haas School of Business (*Haas*) was my Mt. Everest. I wanted to get in, but I figured the odds were lowest with this school. I also picked another nearby University of California (UC) school, a regionally recognized private school, and a local California State University (CSU) school. The CSU school was my *safety* school. To my surprise, I got into all four schools! Berkeley, of course, was last to notify me, so I was on the edge of my seat for several months as acceptances rolled in.

The first class (Microeconomics) was scary and impressive. The professor had memorized all 60 student's names before the class even started. My colleagues were impressive too. Some had accomplished so much in what seemed like so little time. Of course, some of that was posturing, as I later came to find out, but a lot of it was real. I had typically excelled in school. But I soon came to realize that the class was filled with some genuinely gifted people, which is one of the major benefits of an MBA program (especially a better program). The network of colleagues you build may be one of the best benefits you receive from an MBA program (more on that in subsequent sections).

The following are other aspects of MBA programs you should know about before deciding to apply.

Harvard Business Cases

It is almost a stereotype, but one of the foundational elements of teaching in an MBA program is the use of Harvard business cases. Harvard Business School has an entire library of business cases for just about every topic in business school. Professors choose the case that matches the principle they are teaching. Each case starts with a narrative. These narratives contain facts you will need to provide your solution. It is then up to you to do an analysis of the data and provide a solution. Most of these solutions are mathematical in some way. Most require several hours of work and a pretty good understanding of the principles being demonstrated. There is typically just one solution, but infinite ways to get it wrong.

I found most of these business cases to be really difficult, but they usually represented business situations that came from the real world, so their application to business was very relevant. I found the explanation of the solution by the professors to be fascinating.

Class Preparation

Given the caliber of students MBA programs attract, I should not have been surprised at the attention to detail each student paid to homework and preparation. I found my colleagues at Haas showed up ready to impress. In fact, the kind of people top programs attract like to take the spotlight. For those like me who are more comfortable in the background, it was a shock to see the bar was so high for preparation and class participation.

Group Work

Group work is great for getting to know your colleagues, but these assignments were my least favorite aspect of the program. People doing evening MBAs have demanding full-time jobs, usually have families, and are also often involved in their hobbies and interests. Getting a group of people together for a class project was difficult. We often had to meet late at night, and at odd times on the weekend. If you are considering getting an MBA, you will need to consider your tolerance for group work.

Electives

Once your core work is completed, you're able to choose your electives. There are two common approaches to electives. The first is to choose those that will build your knowledge in your chosen career area. There are usually good selections that can help you bolster your skills and knowledge in complementary areas. If you are career-changing, you'll want to follow this strategy to maximize your exposure to the relevant materials in your new career focus.

The other school of thought says that you should pick classes that personally interest you because you only get one chance to go through an MBA program. I regret not taking two classes during my time in school. The first was a real estate class. Real estate had nothing to do with my learning or career objectives, but I have a personal interest in it. To this day, I occasionally see the professor interviewed in print or television, and I kick myself for not taking his class. The other regret was a course where I was more interested in the professor than the subject matter. At the time I was at Haas, we had Janet Yellen (former Chair of the U.S. Federal Reserve, and current U.S. Secretary of the Treasury) teaching an occasional class. At the time, she was Chair of the San Francisco Federal Reserve, and there was always a lot of buzz around her class. When she was promoted, I again regretted not taking her class, even though it was not directly related to my career direction. If you can't tell, I am a fan of taking the electives you find the most interesting. You only get one chance.

Balancing Work, Family, and School

You may be early enough in your career that it may make sense to pause it and dive into school full time. In some cases, it may also make sense if you are interested in switching careers. However, there is a large (and growing) group of students who are hoping to manage a full-time job, family, and school all at the same time. I was one of those students.

At the time I started school, I had a stressful (but not especially prestigious) job that I wanted to leave for something better. The problem was I needed the job because I also had a wife and three kids. During the program, there was no spare time in my life, and if I am being honest, my wife should have received a degree at the end of the program because it affected her as much as me. As you contemplate whether to pursue an MBA, be sure account for the impact to all those around you.

There really is no *balance* in a situation where you are taking on so much at one time. Instead of seeking balance, know that you will have to work harder than you've had to before. You will have the never-ending pressures of school, work, and family continually tugging on you. If you don't have any family attachments, this may not be an issue, but you will still have to sacrifice major aspects your personal life.

What Benefits Does an MBA Really Provide?

There are so many choices for MBA programs that it is impossible to expect that all MBA programs deliver the same benefits, but I believe there are some common benefits that most of them will (and should!) provide. Additionally, I have seen that the benefits I receive from my MBA change as time goes on.

Opening Doors

I'm not going to lie, having an MBA from UC Berkeley has opened a lot of doors for me that I don't believe programs from lower-ranked schools would have opened. I've had recruiters call because of it. I've had hiring manages tell me that it was because of the MBA they were interested in me. However, I have seen this benefit diminish substantially over time. Someone recently out of business school is more interesting to employers than someone who is 10+ years away from it. At that point, it is more about the person's accomplishments than the degree.

I also want to point out that an MBA may open the door, but you have to have the talent in order to walk through it. I've had the degree get me interviews for dream jobs that I wasn't able to land because experience still matters. Getting in the door is a great start, though, and feels good!

Alumni Network

Any college you attend will have an alumni network. When you are considering a school, this may not be one of the top criteria you judge it by, but you will, literally, spend decades as an alumnus of your school of choice. Be sure your fellow alums are going to bolster the value of your degree.

Some schools have excellent alumni networks that can also be leveraged to open doors for you. Having alumni who are recognized leaders in the corporate world is helpful if you are interested in leveraging the prestige of your school for career advancement. As with opening doors, I found these networks are most valuable when you are recently graduated. Alumni have a soft spot for new graduates. Help will be more forthcoming the earlier you are in your career.

Network of Colleagues

There is another network, in addition to the alumni network, that is of great worth to graduates. This is the network of fellow classmates and professors that will grow naturally as you work with them in your classes. Some people are natural networkers, some are not. As you can imagine, those who know how to network reap greater benefits than those of us who don't do it as well. One of my regrets is that I did not push myself to network with my colleagues more. Now that many years have passed, I look at my LinkedIn profile and I still see many of my colleagues, but I have done a middling job of keeping those relationships cultivated. Having a strong network is one of the keys to navigating the competitive corporate environment.

Transitioning Careers

If you are considering changing career tracks, then going back to school can be a useful part of your narrative to prospective employers. If you are in IT and want to change to a career in marketing, it is very hard to get any hiring managers to take you seriously without some kind of hook to get you in the door. An MBA can be an excellent tool for a transition if you focus your MBA electives in your field of choice. This will give you talking points with a potential employer.

There is a brief window within which a career change can make sense to an employer. The first year after graduating is perfect for the switch. Much longer than that, and the story starts to sound thin. If you are thinking of a transition, plan accordingly.

If you are a project or program manager and want to transition to another career, an MBA could be a valuable part of your transition plan. If you are not a project or program manager and want to become one, there are probably better ways to plan your transition. Getting real-world experience and a certification or two will be less intense, less expensive, and likely more effective than an MBA. However, once you are in a project career track, an MBA can unleash meaningful career progression in the field.

Technical Knowledge

Some may pursue an MBA for the actual business knowledge, formulas, and models that are taught so that they can advance their careers, or because they are generally curious about the subject matter. The information taught can be applied in personal life too. Want to learn more about valuing stocks? Or real estate investing? Or how to be an entrepreneur? An

IS AN MBA RIGHT FOR YOU?   163

MBA program can teach you valuable skills in any of these areas for those who may want to work outside of the traditional corporate structure.

If you want to learn about trading stocks, you may be disappointed in what is taught. The program will teach you how to determine whether a company has intrinsic value, but I have not seen an MBA program that concentrates on technical trading or other common trading techniques. That said, I personally believe that understanding company valuation is very important, and I am not alone because Warren Buffet made his fortune by understanding the fundamental value of companies.

Career Advancement

One of the reasons people pursue an MBA is for career advancement in a more traditional corporate environment. They may want to move into management, or move up the management chain to executive-level positions. Many envision sitting at the top of the corporate structure in a CEO role. Getting to the very top of an organization does not require an MBA, but an MBA can help a person unlock nascent talent.

Many people hope to advance beyond individual contributor to a management role. Setting up students for advancement is the bread and butter of a business school.

For project management professionals, this can manifest in a couple of ways. Career advancement can mean a title change and taking on larger, more complex projects. It can also mean becoming a people manager within a program leadership structure such as a PMO. An MBA will set you apart from your colleagues. That said, there are some caveats to consider before starting an MBA if this is your primary motivation.

First, if you want to move up within your current organization, be sure that management within your organization understands and support your decision. Better yet, you may want to pre-negotiate what happens after you get your degree. In my case, my immediate manager supported my plan, and I was able to tap into the company's tuition reimbursement program for a (small) offset to the overall cost. What I hadn't done was talk with my manager (or any other leaders) about what my future would look like at completion. It turns out I got exactly what I negotiated—nothing. To be fair, the company was struggling, and I was laid off near the time of graduation, so any expectations would have been void anyway. However, I stand by the idea of understanding the reward before signing up for the work.

Second, if you expect to switch organizations to get the role or compensation you want, start setting the stage as soon as possible. Use your status as a student to develop relationships with key people at your company of choice. By using the *student* angle, you are much less threatening to those you reach out to who get regularly hit up for jobs. Use contacts within your program to help you meet the right people. Use LinkedIn or other tools to ask for an informational interview where you can ask those key contacts about what it's like to work within the company. Then, as you get closer to graduation, use your contacts to find a way in.

Finally, be aware of the tier of company you are currently in and the tier you want to work for. For example, if you currently work for a small regional company, you will have to work hard to get in to a Goldman Sachs or Google caliber company, so really play up the student angle to start building those relationships.

Confidence

This may not seem like an obvious reason to go to business school, but I know that many of my classmates (and myself) felt just a little better about ourselves upon completion of the program. Confidence in the workplace is critical for advancement. In addition to a general boost of confidence, there is a more specific kind of confidence that can come to graduates. As you learn about all aspects of a way business runs, those of us who interact with departments across the company (as many project and program managers *do*) can talk to cross-functional colleagues with better understanding, which results in more confidence. I consider the cross-functional knowledge I gained in business school to be one of the greatest benefits I personally received. Every day as I talk to my colleagues, I am able to draw on either direct knowledge from the program or the residual confidence gained.

Ways of Thinking

As you move through an MBA program, you learn from experts in finance, accounting, human resources, marketing, operations, economics, and other disciplines. Each of these disciplines uses a unique lens to view business problems and opportunities. The intense exposure to all of these areas you receive will open your mind to ideas, frameworks, and ways of thinking that are of great value.

I recall doing an exercise in an operations class where we walked through every step of making a batch of cookies. We broke down each step to its basic form. We assigned an expected time to each step, then started to look for ways to make the process more efficient. I remember sitting back during the experience and feeling that I was changed. I started to look at the simplest of activities in my life and breaking them down, then rebuilding them. Even now, I think about simple movements I make and wonder if I can do it better. This kind of thinking hit me so powerfully because I'd never considered it before. This is the power of an MBA. You will come out a stronger, more critical thinker.

Starting Your Own Company (Entrepreneurship)

For those who desire to strike out on their own and get away from the grind of corporate life, an MBA can be a catalyst for enacting that change. Entrepreneurs have to take on responsibilities around taxes, liability, finance, and legal issues that corporate project and program managers normally do not. An MBA can help you navigate some of those new responsibilities, but in an even more powerful way, an MBA from a respected school can help investors and potential clients be at ease with your professional capabilities. To those wishing to start their own company, I strongly suggest considering an MBA. MBA programs are a breeding ground for innovative thinking and entrepreneurial spirit. A good MBA program will not only teach you valuable skills but connect you to like-minded students and alumni who will help you on your entrepreneurial journey.

One of the motivations for me to enter the program was that I wanted to see if I had what it took to start my own business. Ultimately, I decided to stay the course on my career and not risk my family's financial future. Sometimes, I think about what might have been different, but I am very at peace (and very grateful to the program) for the decision I was able to make.

Some project and program managers looking to move out of the corporate world may not want to start a company; they may simply want to become an independent consultant. While it is not necessary to get an

MBA to become independent, it can help. All of the entrepreneurial skills taught are directly transferrable to independent consulting.

What Tier of School to Target?

When I was applying to programs, my methodology was simple: Get into the best program possible. In hindsight, I believe this was a naive way of thinking. I might not have chosen Haas, given what I know now. It's not that there is anything wrong with Haas; it's an amazing program, and I recommend it for candidates who can really make the benefits outweigh the costs. Let's get clear on what the benefits and drawbacks of the various tiers are:

Top Tier

Top tier means programs that are highly ranked by *U.S. News & World Report* (U.S. programs), *Financial Times* (global programs), and other reputable independent assessors. If your school of choice is in the top 20 of one of these lists, you're targeting top tier. Be aware that there are different rankings for full-time, part-time, and executive MBA programs, so pay attention to which program the list is assessing.

Table 10.1 contains a summary of the pros and cons of attending a top-tier school.

The *pros* listed are of little value if you are not the right personality to take advantage of them. For example, as I've said before, I am not a great networker. I should have thought more carefully about the program I chose because the excellent Haas network was somewhat wasted

Table 10.1 Pros and cons of top-tier schools

Pros	Cons
Excellent education	Cost, cost, cost (and maybe long-term debt)
Strong networking opportunities	Big time commitment during program
Opens doors	
Strong alumni network	
Nationally recognized professors	

on me. This decreased the benefit of my MBA compared to the cost. Be thoughtful about what level of school you select, not everyone can take full advantage of a top-tier program.

Mid-Tier

By mid-tier, I mean those programs that are lower on the national or global rankings, or rely on strong regional reputation. These are solid schools with strong professors but without the reputation of top-tier schools. For mid-tier schools, look at the size and quality of the alumni network, the services offered (such as career services), employment placement rate, and reputation within your focus area (i.e., are they known as a good marketing school). Also, the reputation of the university can vary from the reputation of the MBA program. Look at both.

Finally, we know that top-tier schools will cost a lot, but mid-tier schools can be costly too, especially when private. It's possible to get a really good education at a good price, you just have to look. It is also possible to get a middling education for at a high cost. Do your research. Table 10.2 shows the pros and cons for mid-tier schools.

Lower Tier/Online

This is a tricky tier to navigate, but the reward could be an excellent education at a great price. Lower-tier schools are probably not on any ranked list. They may be state schools, regional private schools, or online. They probably won't have a strong alumni network or strong support programs. However, if you are in a position where achievement of the degree means more than the reputation of the school, this may be the best choice for you.

Table 10.2 Pros and cons of mid-tier schools

Pros	Cons
Solid education	Cost (maybe)
May be good return on investment	Opens fewer doors
Can be used for a career change	Limited name recognition
May have a good alumni network (do your research)	

Table 10.3 Pros and cons of lower-tier schools

Pros	Cons
Cost/bang-for-buck	Alumni network
Convenience (online, local)	Opens fewer doors
Can be used for a career change	No reputation

I recognize that by lumping online programs with lower-tier schools, I risk offending many people. I actually believe that you can get a good education online. But I remain unconvinced that online programs can forge the kind of peer relationships an in-person program can. Additionally, I remain surprised at how expensive they are compared to in-person programs, making it harder for me to see the justification. I want to call out that an online program from a school that *also* has a traditional program may make for a better value proposition.

One bonus for online programs is that they may be gaining in value. Given the enormous shift to *online everything* since the Covid-19 pandemic, the prior stigma of online programs may be diminishing. If you are considering an online program, be sure to watch for more traditional schools to go online. You may be able to get the best of all worlds by combining the reputational strength and alumni network of a mid-tier (or better) school with the convenience of an online program.

If it seems like I am down on lower-tier schools, I am not. In fact, I think I may have been better served by a lower-tier school. Here's why: When I was freshly graduated, I was careful to mention to people that I recently completed an MBA program, and this allowed me to work in the fact that I went to UC Berkeley (jerk alert). Now that I have more than a decade behind me, I almost never bring it up. I have developed an intense dislike for people who drop the name of the snooty school they graduated from. Without the name-dropping part of the program, value disappears. Table 10.3 shows the pros and cons of lower-tier/online schools.

Does an MBA Still Have Value?

There has been a lot of public debate about the value of higher education in recent years. This debate, coupled with concerns over the high loads of student loan debt, has caused many to question whether the cost of advanced degrees is worth it. This debate is still raging, and I don't know if anything definitive will ever be decided. I definitely have some thoughts that may be of value to you as you make your decision.

The democratization of education (pushing it down from the elite to everyone) is great for individuals and, I believe, society as a whole. But value is rarely created out of nowhere. I believe part of the value derived from this availability is a general devaluation of advanced degrees. Do I believe the MBA is as valuable as it once was? No. The title MBA used to carry a real cachet. It's not the same anymore. Do I believe the MBA still has value? Absolutely. For some, it may be a catalyst to an amazing new career or a rapid climb up the career ladder. I also believe, as I've characterized earlier, that MBAs are not for everyone in every circumstance.

I think the right question to be asking is "Will an MBA have value *to me?*" This is a more difficult question today than decades ago, but it is worth figuring out. I'm hoping that with the advice in this book and with some research, you can answer this question for yourself.

When Is the Right Time?

I really want to be able to tell you to follow your dream to get an MBA, no matter the time and circumstance, but I can't. Due to the large investment of time and money, there is a time payback horizon that needs to be analyzed. The earlier in your career you are, the longer the payoff window, the more return on investment of your time and money.

In the spirit of transparency, there is no data underlying this opinion other than my own experience, and those of my friends and colleagues who feel roughly the same. But I believe the concept holds up well to the laws of common sense: the greatest value is derived early, and the benefits derived from the degree decrease over time. So, as you contemplate your decision, be sure you leave enough time to get your payback.

I decided to get an MBA when I was 33 years old. By the time I finished (Haas is a three-year program for evening/weekend students), I was 37. I was slightly older than the average age, but not by much. I recall one student who was 48. He was the oldest I am aware of in my cohort. When I think about his payoff window, I question whether he would be able to recoup the value of the effort and cost, assuming retirement around age 65. I can say that the payoff for my MBA is still accumulating (albeit more slowly now), but I would not have wanted to start my program much later than I did. I don't know that payoff would have made sense. So, as I stated previously, think carefully before pursuing an MBA, especially if you are more mature.

Would You Do It Again?

This is an $84,000 question for me. More than that, actually, due to the costs of the time invested and the impact on my family. When I think about what I was earning at the time and what I am earning now, there is definitely a positive progression. The problem is, I am not sure that I couldn't have had the same successes on my own. I'll never know how much of my career success after the MBA is directly correlated to the degree.

When people ask if I would I do it over again, I warn them that the answer is a long one, and they may want to sit down. I affirmatively believe the skills I learned (and have shared in this book) are of enormous value to anyone in project and program management. I also believe that the confidence and exposure to all aspects of business gave me a great foundation on which to build a stronger career. I may have gotten there alone, but it was not guaranteed.

I also believe that had I not chosen to pursue an MBA, a part of me would have always wondered whether I missed out. I am sure I would have felt some regret, and the cost of regret can be considerable.

When I take everything into account, I can say I *would* get an MBA again. I would have applied several years earlier so that the impact on my wife and family would have been less. I might have even considered stopping my career and pursuing the degree full time.

Whether I would have gone to Haas again is harder for me to parse. I benefited most from the education and the opening of doors. I could have gotten the education from virtually any reputable school. If I pursued a regionally recognized school (and I got into one), it would likely have had the same door-opening power, considering I have stayed in the same regional market most of my career. I don't think attending a school like Haas was necessary for me to achieve the benefits I've accrued.

Next Steps

If you are considering an MBA, congratulations—you are asking a very important question! I know that an MBA pursued at the right time and in the right way will not only make you a stronger project management professional but could open doors to many other exciting professional adventures. I hope you will take the following steps:

1. Start using the tools and techniques explained in this book to become acquainted with key MBA teachings. Under any circumstance, this can help your career.
2. Determine the ways an MBA is likely to help you, given your natural strengths. Are you a good networker? Great! Find a school with a good reputation and strong alumni pool because you will gain great value from them.
3. Research schools in your area and online. Look at reputations and rankings. Look at costs and types of programs offered. Talk to graduates. Find the programs that best fit your criteria.
4. Do the math. Figure out both the direct costs (tuition, books, etc.) and the indirect costs (What are you giving up? How is it impacting your family?). Then look at the benefits. Be realistic—how will you really benefit?
5. If the math works and you have support from your family and employer (if doing a part-time program), then congratulations; you're on the path to getting your MBA!

Notes

Chapter 1

1. Porter (1980).
2. Doti and Iannoccone (May 04, 2020).

Chapter 2

1. Staff Investopedia (2021).
2. "Opportunity Cost." (2021).
3. Staff Investopedia (2021).
4. Kenton (2021).
5. Hayes (2021).
6. Banton (2021).
7. PMI (2017).
8. Kruse (2021).

Chapter 3

1. "Fiscal Year." (2021).
2. Fern (n.d.).
3. Folger (2021).
4. Hayes (2021).
5. Fern (2021).
6. Fayard (2021).
7. Liberto (2021).
8. Kenton (2021).
9. Hayes (n.d.).
10. Murphy (2021).
11. Fern (2021).
12. Fern (2021).
13. Fernando and Khartit (2021).
14. Columbia University's Mailman School of Public Health (2021).
15. Nofsinger (2021).

Chapter 4

1. Kenton (2021).
2. Tuovila (2021).

Chapter 5

1. Kenton (2021).
2. "6.1.3. What Is Process Control?" (2021).
3. Severins (2015).

Chapter 6

1. "What Is Marketing? — The Definition of Marketing — AMA." (2021).
2. "Coca-Cola: Brand Value 2019." (2021).
3. Radhika (2021).
4. Dorie (2021).
5. Schneider (2018).
6. Clement (2021).
7. Wurmser (2021).

Chapter 7

1. "MBA Applications and Aspirations Report 2018: An Overview." (2018).

Chapter 8

1. "Who Said 'the Only Thing Constant Is Change'?" (2021).
2. Kotter (2012).
3. Kotter (2012).
4. French and Raven (1959).
5. Maslow (1943).
6. Herzberg (2003).
7. Vroom (1964).
8. Trump and Schwartz (2009).
9. "About the Harvard Negotiation Project." (2018).
10. Fisher, William, and Bruce (2011).
11. "Business Ethics." (2021).

Chapter 9

1. Winch (2021).
2. Hersey and Blanchard (1969).
3. "Dr. Meredith Belbin." (2021).
4. "Wiley Everything DiSC Solutions." (2021).
5. Fayard (2021).
6. "The Myers & Briggs Foundation." (2021).
7. Henkel, Haley, Bourdeau, and Marion (2019).
8. "The Myers & Briggs Foundation - The 16 MBTI® Types." (2021).
9. Maxwell (1960).
10. "A Guide to Belbin Team Roles." (2021).

References

"About the Harvard Negotiation Project." 2018. *PON - Program on Negotiation at Harvard Law School* (blog). www.pon.harvard.edu/research_projects/harvard-negotiation-project/hnp/ (accessed November 07, 2018).

"MBA Applications and Aspirations Report 2018: An Overview." 2018. *TopMBA.Com.* www.topmba.com/admissions/mba-applications-and-aspirations-report-2018-overview (accessed February 22, 2018).

"Business Ethics." 2021. https://dictionary.cambridge.org/us/dictionary/english/business-ethics (accessed February 27, 2021).

"Coca-Cola: Brand Value 2019." 2021. *Statista.* www.statista.com/statistics/326065/coca-cola-brand-value/ (accessed February 27, 2021).

"Dr. Meredith Belbin." 2021. www.belbin.com/about/dr-meredith-belbin/ (accessed February 27, 2021).

"Fiscal Year." 2021. https://dictionary.cambridge.org/us/dictionary/english/fiscal-year (accessed February 24, 2021).

"Opportunity Cost." 2021. dictionary.cambridge.org/us/dictionary/english/opportunity-cost (accessed February 23, 2021).

"The Myers & Briggs Foundation - The 16 MBTI® Types." 2021. www.myersbriggs.org/my-mbti-personality-type/mbti-basics/the-16-mbti-types.htm (accessed February 27, 2021).

"The Myers & Briggs Foundation." 2021. www.myersbriggs.org/ (accessed February 27, 2021).

"What Is Marketing?—The Definition of Marketing—AMA." 2021. *American Marketing Association.* www.ama.org/the-definition-of-marketing-what-is-marketing/ (accessed February 27, 2021).

"Wiley Everything DiSC Solutions." 2021. www.everythingdisc.com/Home.aspx (accessed February 27, 2021).

"6.1.3. What Is Process Control?" 2021. www.itl.nist.gov/div898/handbook/pmc/section1/pmc13.htm (accessed April 03, 2021).

"A Guide to Belbin Team Roles." 2021. *Belbin North America* (blog). https://belbinnorthamerica.com/a-guide-to-belbin-team-roles/ (accessed April 11, 2021).

"Who Said 'the Only Thing Constant Is Change'?" 2021. *Reference.Com.* www.reference.com/world-view/said-only-thing-constant-change-d50c0532e714e12b (accessed April 11, 2021).

Banton, C. 2021. "Complementary Goods." *Investopedia.* www.investopedia.com/terms/c/complement.asp (accessed February 23, 2021).

Clark, D. 2021. "How Raising Prices Can Increase Your Sales." *Forbes.* www.forbes.com/sites/dorieclark/2012/02/23/how-raising-prices-can-increase-your-sales/ (accessed February 27, 2021).

Clement, J. 2021. "Mobile Percentage of Website Traffic 2020." *Statista.* www.statista.com/statistics/277125/share-of-website-traffic-coming-from-mobile-devices/ (accessed February 27, 2021).

Columbia University's Mailman School of Public Health. 2021. "Global Study Confirms Influential Theory Behind Loss Aversion." *ScienceDaily.* www.sciencedaily.com/releases/2020/05/200518144913.htm (accessed February 24, 2021).

Doti, J., and L. Iannoccone. May 04, 2020. "Why You Can't Find Rubbing Alcohol." *Wall Street Journal,* www.wsj.com/articles/why-you-cant-find-rubbing-alcohol-11588629519

Fayard, J.V., Ph.D. 2021. "Your Favorite Personality Test Is Probably Bogus." *Psychology Today.* www.psychologytoday.com/blog/people-are-strange/2019/09/your-favorite-personality-test-is-probably-bogus (accessed March 30, 2021).

Fern, J. (n.d.). "Balance Sheet." *Investopedia.* https://www.investopedia.com/terms/b/balancesheet.asp (accessed August 17, 2021).

Fern, J. 2021. "Equity." *Investopedia.* www.investopedia.com/terms/e/equity.asp (accessed February 24, 2021).

Fern, J. 2021. "Equity." *Investopedia.* www.investopedia.com/terms/e/equity.asp (accessed April 11, 2021).

Fernando, J., and K. Khartit. 2021. "Internal Rate of Return (IRR)." *Investopedia.* www.investopedia.com/terms/i/irr.asp (accessed February 24, 2021).

Fernando, J., and K. Khartit. 2021. "Net Present Value (NPV)." *Investopedia.* www.investopedia.com/terms/n/npv.asp (accessed February 24, 2021).

Fernando, J., and K. Khartit. 2021. "Return on Investment (ROI) Definition." *Investopedia.* www.investopedia.com/terms/r/returnoninvestment.asp (accessed February 24, 2021).

Fisher, R., L.U. William, and P. Bruce. 2011. *Getting to yes: Negotiating Agreement without Giving in.* Penguin.

Folger, J. 2021. "What Is an Asset?" *Investopedia.* www.investopedia.com/ask/answers/12/what-is-an-asset.asp (accessed February 24, 2021).

French, J., and B. Raven. 1959. *The Bases of Social Power.*

Hayes, A. n.d. "Gross Profit." *Investopedia.* https://www.investopedia.com/terms/g/grossprofit.asp (accessed August 17, 2021).

Hayes, A. 2021. "How Substitutes Work." *Investopedia,* www.investopedia.com/terms/s/substitute.asp (accessed February 23, 2021).

Hayes, A. 2021. "Liability." *Investopedia.* www.investopedia.com/terms/l/liability.asp (accessed February 24, 2021).

Henkel, T.G., G. Haley, D.T. Bourdeau, and J. Marion. 2019. "An Insight to Project Manager Personality Traits." *Graziadio Business Review* 22, no. 2, p. 1. https://gbr.pepperdine.edu/2019/08/an-insight-to-project-manager-personality-traits/

Hersey, P., and K.H. Blanchard. 1969. "Life Cycle Theory of Leadership." *Training and Development Journal* 23, no. 5, pp. 26–34.

Herzberg, F. 2003. "One More Time: How Do You Motivate Employees?" *Harvard Business Review*. hbr.org/2003/01/one-more-time-how-do-you-motivate-employees (accessed January 01, 2003).

Kenton, W. 2021. "Financial Accounting." *Investopedia*. www.investopedia.com/terms/f/financialaccounting.asp (accessed February 27, 2021).

Kenton, W. 2021. "How Enterprise Risk Management (ERM) Works." *Investopedia*. www.investopedia.com/terms/e/enterprise-risk-management.asp (accessed February 27, 2021).

Kenton, W. 2021. "Net Income (NI)." *Investopedia*. www.investopedia.com/terms/n/netincome.asp (accessed February 24, 2021).

Kenton, W. 2021. "Supply." *Investopedia*. www.investopedia.com/terms/s/supply.asp (accessed February 23, 2021).

Kruse, K. 2021. "The 80/20 Rule And How It Can Change Your Life." *Forbes*, www.forbes.com/sites/kevinkruse/2016/03/07/80-20-rule/ (accessed April 7, 2021).

Kotter, J.P. 2012. *Leading Change*. Harvard Business Press.

Kotter, J.P. 2021. "Accelerate!." *Harvard Business Review* 90, no. 11, pp. 44–52.

Liberto, D. 2021. "Expense Definition." *Investopedia*. www.investopedia.com/terms/e/expense.asp (accessed February 24, 2021).

Maslow, A.H. 1943. "A Theory of Human Motivation." *Psychological Review* 50, no. 4, pp. 370–396.

Maxwell, J.C. 1960. *The 5 Levels of Leadership*. New York, NY: Center Street.

Murphy, C.B. 2021. "Understanding the Cash Flow Statement." *Investopedia*. www.investopedia.com/investing/what-is-a-cash-flow-statement/ (accessed February 24, 2021).

Nofsinger, J., Ph.D. 2021. "Familiarity Bias PART I: What Is It?" *Psychology Today*. www.psychologytoday.com/blog/mind-my-money/200807/familiarity-bias-part-i-what-is-it (accessed February 24, 2021).

PMI. 2017. Project Management Job Growth and Talent Gap 2017–2027.

Porter, M.E 1980. "Competitive Strategy: Techniques for Analyzing Industries and Competitors." *Editorial Free Pr*.

Radhika, D. 2021. "Council Post: The One Marketing Truism You Cannot Ignore: Perception Is Reality." *Forbes*. www.forbes.com/sites/forbescommunicationscouncil/2018/05/29/the-one-marketing-truism-you-cannot-ignore-perception-is-reality/ (accessed February 27, 2021).

Schneider, M. 2018. "Report: PR Pros Outnumber Journalists by a 6-to-1 Ratio." *PR Daily* (blog). www.prdaily.com/report-pr-pros-outnumber-journalists-by-a-6-to-1-ratio/ (accessed September 19, 2018).

Severins, J. 2015. "The Amazing Supply Chain of Your Morning Coffee - Inventory & Supply Chain Blog." *All Things Supply Chain.* www.allthingssupplychain.com/the-amazing-supply-chain-of-your-morning-coffee/ (accessed August 31, 2021).

Staff Investopedia. 2021. "Utility Definition." *Investopedia,* www.investopedia.com/terms/u/utility.asp (accessed February 23, 2021).

Staff, Investopedia. 2021. "Demand Definition." *Investopedia,* www.investopedia.com/terms/d/demand.asp (accessed February 23, 2021).

Trump, D.J., and T. Schwartz. 2009. *Trump: The Art of the Deal.* Ballantine Books.

Tuovila, A. 2021. "Managerial Accounting Definition." *Investopedia.* www.investopedia.com/terms/m/managerialaccounting.asp (accessed February 27, 2021).

Vroom, V.H. 1964. *Work and Motivation.*

Winch, G., Ph.D. 2021. "Can Leadership Be Learned or Are You Born With It?" *Psychology Today.* www.psychologytoday.com/blog/the-squeaky-wheel/201502/can-leadership-be-learned-or-are-you-born-it (accessed February 27, 2021).

Wurmser, Y. 2021. "Apps Far Outpace Browsers in US Adults' Mobile Time Spent." *Insider Intelligence.* www.emarketer.com/content/the-majority-of-americans-mobile-time-spent-takes-place-in-apps (accessed February 27, 2021).

About the Author

Brad Clark, MBA, PMP, has been managing projects, programs, and people for nearly 25 years.

He received his Bachelor of Arts from Brigham Young University in 1994, and his Master of Science from Florida State University in 1996. In 2007, he received his Master's in Business Administration (MBA) from U.C. Berkeley's Haas School of Business. He has been Project Management Professional (PMP)-certified since 2008.

His program management career started in 1997 and has included work at small start-ups where the company's future was tied to the success of his projects, all the way to large, multinational companies where his work impacted tens of thousands of employees. He has managed the Project Management Offices (PMOs) at three different companies. He has hired dozens of project and program managers and knows what it takes to advance in this profession.

Brad's professional passion manifests at the junction of business and technology where he can apply his learnings from his MBA to real-world technology challenges faced by companies. Brad lives in Springville, Utah, with his wife Colleen, to whom he's been married for more than 28 years. They have four daughters, one son, five chickens, four ducks, two dogs, and too many fish to count.

Index

9 781637 421253